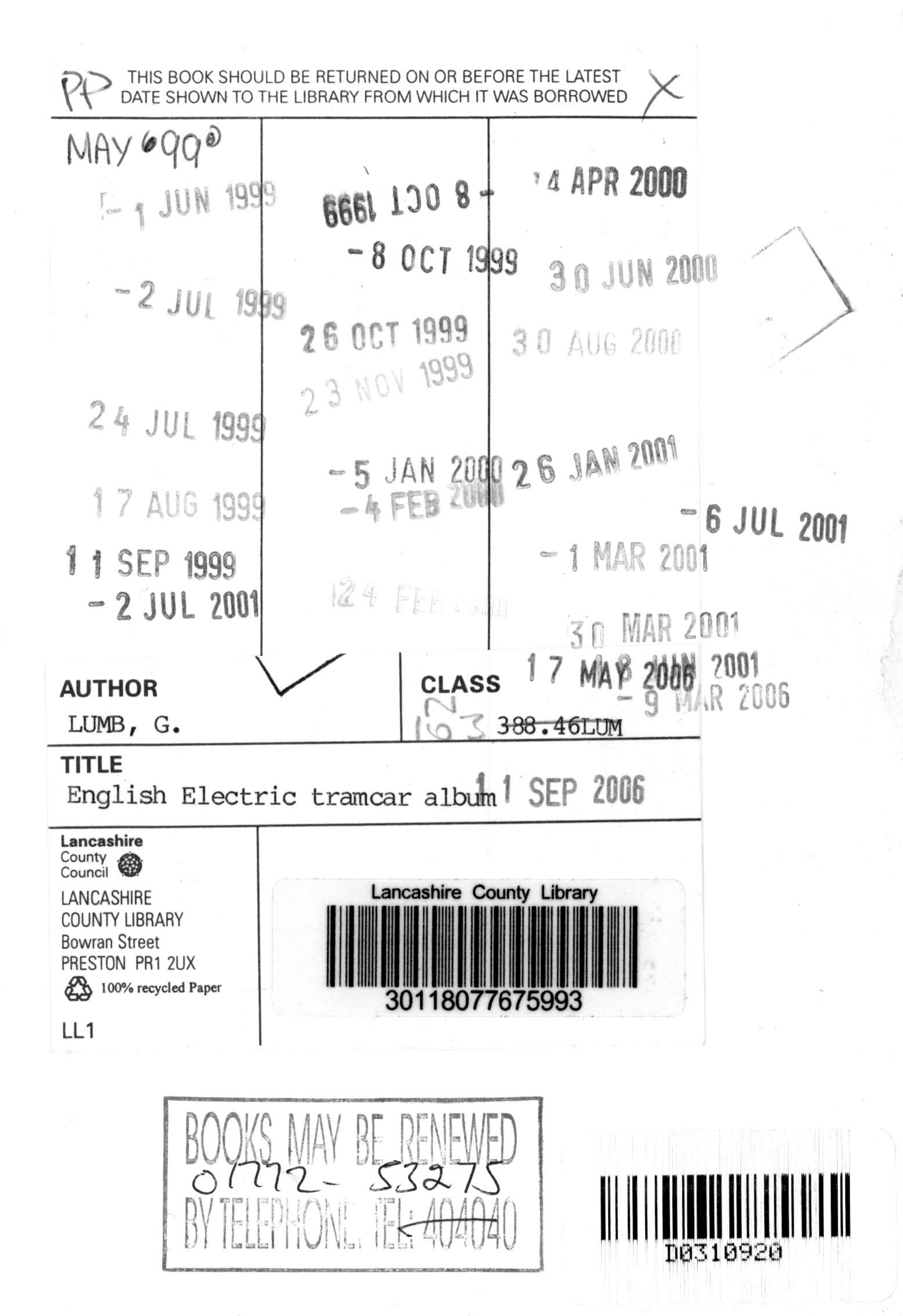
THIS BOOK SHOULD BE RETURNED ON OR BEFORE THE LATEST DATE SHOWN TO THE LIBRARY FROM WHICH IT WAS BORROWED
AUTHOR
LUMB, G.
CLASS
388.46LUM
TITLE
English Electric tramcar album
Lancashire County Council
LANCASHIRE COUNTY LIBRARY
Bowran Street
PRESTON PR1 2UX
100% recycled Paper
LL1
Lancashire County Library
30118077675993

English Electric Tramcar Album

ROCHDALE CORPORATIO

English Electric Tramcar Album

Geoff Lumb

First published 1998

ISBN 0 7110 2613 0

Published by Ian Allan Publishing

an imprint of Ian Allan Publishing Ltd, Terminal House, Station Approach, Shepperton, Surrey TW17 8AS.
Printed by Ian Allan Printing Ltd, Riverdene Business Park, Molesey Road, Hersham, Surrey KT12 4RG.

Code: 9808/

Contents

Front cover: Sunderland car No 30 is seen at Seaburn Terminus in October 1954. This car built in 1931 was originally Huddersfield No 141 and was one of eight cars sold by Huddersfield to Sunderland in 1938. *Roy Brook*

Back cover: Aberdeen car No 140 was photographed in service in August 1955. *Roy Brook*

Half title: Sunderland Corporation purchased four single-deck combination cars in 1902 (Fleet Nos 52-5) with ER&TCW-built bodies mounted on Brill 21E trucks. Car No 52 is seen here. *E. Hoole*

Title page: When Rochdale Corporation introduced electric tramways in 1902, its first tramcars included double-deck open-top bogie car No 2 built by ER&TCW and mounted on Brill 22E bogies. *E. Hoole*

Above: Edinburgh & District Tramways Co Ltd purchased 20 new open-top cable trams in 1903 from ER&TCW, Fleet Nos 209-28. Car No 209 is seen outside the works. The cable system was taken over by Edinburgh Corporation Tramways in June 1919. *E. Hoole*

Acknowledgements

Of the principal sources of material consulted for this book, the first is the National Tramway Museum, Crich, Derbyshire, where Rosy Thacker allowed access to the museum's extensive library. The library contains various customer index cards, specification sheets for electrical equipment and specifications issued to the car builder. These cards, salvaged from the English Electric Phoenix Works at Bradford by C. T. Humpidge, have been an invaluable source of information on the activities of UEC, DK and EE at Preston. Rosy also provided copies of countless articles and documents.

The Lancashire Record Office, Bow Lane, Preston, allowed access to the various files and documents of the companies which Dick, Kerr took over or absorbed in 1917. These companies included United Electric Car Co Ltd, G. F. Milnes & Co Ltd, English Electric Manufacturing Co Ltd, Electric Railway & Tramway Carriage Works Ltd, and also British Electric Car Co Ltd.

The surviving official photographs from GEC Alsthom Traction Ltd, covering tramcars built at Preston between 1900-40, have been made available via David Beilby. The library at

Below: Bolton Corporation No 82 was one of five balcony cars supplied by ER&TCW in 1903. *ER&TCW*

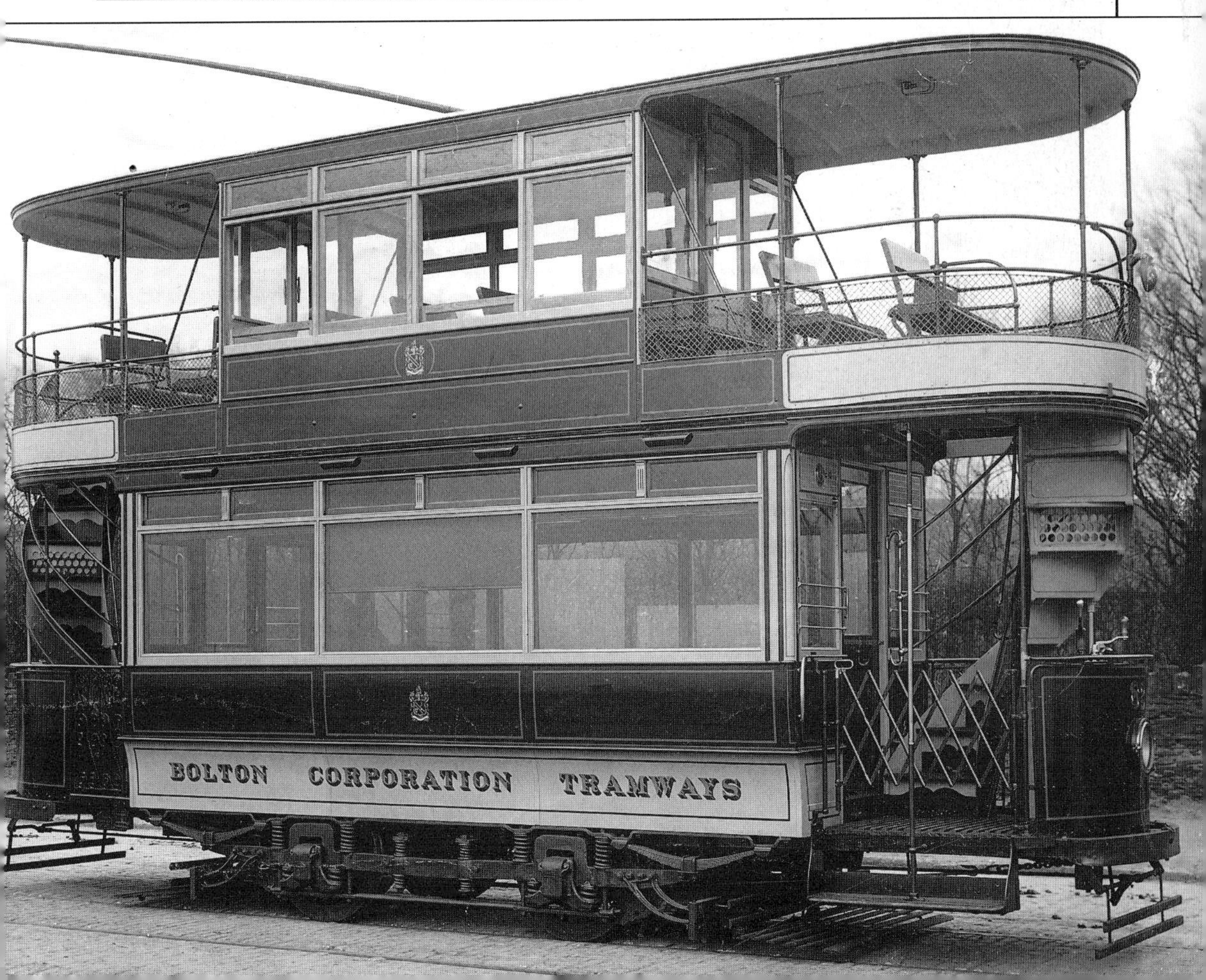

Ian Allan Publishing Ltd, where copies of *The Electric Railway and Tramway Journal* etc have been examined, has also been useful. Other works consulted include the many published fleet histories, which have helped to piece together the many facts about Preston-built tramcars.

Others deserving special mention are Leeds City Council's Patent Library in York Road, John M. Aldridge, G. H. F. Atkins, Roy Brook, F. P. Groves, D. Harvey, Chris Heaps, R. Marshall, Dr M. Mitchell, W. Montgomery, A. D. Packer, D. J. Smithies, J. Soper and Chris Taylor, many of whom have assisted in locating material to help produce this record of the English Electric Company's tramcar production at Preston and in making available photographs at acceptable reproduction fees within the publisher's budget.

Special thanks to my daughter, Clare, for her invaluable help in transcribing my script to disk, and to M. Bray, industrial photographer, who provided the professional skills to achieve superb prints from blue dyeline prints. I am also grateful to P. Waller and N. Grant at Ian Allan Ltd for their patience and help in producing this book.

Last, but not least, to my wife, Ethel, for her patience when books, files, records and photographs for this book took over the front room!

Above: Nelson Corporation operated three bogie combination cars (Nos 7, 8 and 9) from ER&TCW purchased in 1903-4, the open sections being for smokers. *E. Hoole*

Right: Burnley Corporation No 40 was one of eight single-deck bogie cars supplied in 1903 by ER&TCW. The 44-seat cars were mounted on Brill 27G bogies. *ER&TCW*

Introduction

This book is the result of interests going back over 50 years, when travel by public transport was the norm. In my home town of Huddersfield, trolleybuses had replaced the tram, with the eight luxurious tramcars being sold to Sunderland in 1938. Visits to Sunderland in 1953 and 1954 enabled the author to travel on these cars, which still looked modern when compared with others elsewhere. Efforts by my lifelong friend, D. J. Smithies, in October 1954 to find financial support to preserve one of these English Electric-built cars failed. Many other tramcars built in Preston were seen during visits to Aberdeen, Blackpool, Edinburgh, Leeds, Llandudno and Stockport.

The purchase for a preservation project in 1972 of the remains of a 1928 Huddersfield-built Karrier motorbus fitted with an English Electric-built body with a clerestory roof, resembling the 1928 Pantograph cars at Blackpool, helped to rekindle interest in the body-building activities of the English Electric Co Ltd.

Whilst writing *British Trolleybuses 1911-1972*, published in 1995, I unearthed a great deal of new information about the English Electric Co Ltd and its Preston works which had produced more tramcar bodies than any other works in Britain. The publication of *The Dick Kerr Story* by J. H. Price in 1993 covered in depth the activities at Preston up to the formation of the English Electric Co Ltd in December 1918. I hope that readers find my interpretation of the surviving records, which are unfortunately incomplete, to be as interesting for the years from 1918.

I have endeavoured to provide an overview which gives credit to the products designed and built by the thousands of craftsmen who worked at Strand Road, Preston, from the outbreak of war in 1914 through the boom and lean years of the 1920s to the depression in the 1930s, producing tramcars for a potential market diminishing year by year. Due to the widespread introduction of electricity for light and power to domestic and industrial users, the need for a tramway system to provide the base load for the local power station diminished, and many of the smaller tramway systems found it more economical to switch to the cheaper and more flexible motorbus than to borrow capital to modernise and purchase new tramcars.

It is opportune to remind readers that the Electric Railway & Tramway Carriage Works Ltd moved its registered office to Strand Road on 14 December 1898 — almost 100 years ago.

As a tribute to all these craftsmen, I have endeavoured to include illustrations of all the tramcar orders received by English Electric Co Ltd from British customers.

Geoff Lumb
Huddersfield
March 1998

Below: Salford Corporation placed in service 10 single-deck combination cars mounted on Brill 22E bogies. The cars, numbered 151-60, were built by ER&TCW in 1905 and survived in service in this form until 1912 when they were withdrawn. The equipment was reused in a further 10 cars built by Brush in 1913-4. *E. Hoole*

Below right: London United Electric Tramways purchased 40 trams from the United Electric Car Co in 1906 (Fleet Nos 301-40) fitted with 'Robinson' staircases. Sir James Clifton Robinson was the Managing Director of the LUET. The cars were mounted on Brill 22E trucks. *UEC*

1 Historical Background

When English Electric Co Ltd was formed on 14 December 1918, one of the constituent parts was the Dick, Kerr and Co Ltd manufacturing works in Preston.

In 1897, Dick, Kerr & Co, a major contractor for new railway and tramway schemes with extensive works in Kilmarnock, was having to subcontract the manufacture of tramcars to other builders. John Kerr, one of the partners, encouraged a group of businessmen to set up two new companies to exploit the growing interest in the electrification of tramways.

The first company, registered on 25 April 1898, was The English Electric Railway & Tramway Carriage Works Ltd. It was formed to manufacture tramway and railway cars, vehicles for light railways, and acquired the North of England Railway Carriage & Iron Works premises at Strand Road, Preston. These premises had been unoccupied since 1880 and became the registered offices for the company on 14 December 1898. Known as the East Works, they were opened in March 1899.

The second company, initially called the Equipment Syndicate Ltd, erected a new

works on the other side of Strand Road. Known as the West Works, they were completed in June 1900. In November 1900, these works were resold to the English Electric Manufacturing Co Ltd, a new company registered to manufacture all kinds of electrical equipment. Meanwhile, on 24 August 1899, a third company was registered as Dick, Kerr & Co Ltd to carry on business as manufacturers of and dealers in rail and tramway appliances, and apparatus of every description.

All these companies had two common directors — John Kerr and George Flett — who since 1885 had worked together at Dick, Kerr & Co after W. B. Dick started devoting more time to his other business interests, which included W. B. Dick & Co oil merchants. In 1903, Dick, Kerr & Co Ltd absorbed completely the English Electric Manufacturing Co Ltd following a share exchange.

By 1904, the tramcar manufacturing industry was faced with overcapacity problems and some companies were forced into bankruptcy, with others reducing prices to obtain work. In order to stabilise the industry, a group of people from Dick, Kerr & Co Ltd, Metropolitan Carriage & Wagon Co Ltd and British Electric Car Co Ltd formed a syndicate to purchase the Hadley works of G. F. Milnes & Co Ltd. This group, the Castle Car Syndicate, was able to protect the interests of the various shareholders.

Tramcar production would be continued at Preston, and ER&TCW Ltd was renamed The United Electric Car Co Ltd, in 1905, with motor omnibus bodies now being included in the items to be manufactured. The new company then purchased the Castle Car Works at Hadley from the syndicate for £80,000 — £65,000 from a cash payment and the remaining £15,000 in shares. The British Electric Car Works at Trafford Park, Manchester, was purchased for £85,000.

The various companies taken over continued as non-trading subsidiaries of the United Electric Car Co Ltd until March 1917. These were Electric Railway & Tramway Carriage Works Ltd, G. F. Milnes & Co Ltd, and British Electric Car Co Ltd.

Below: Stockport Corporation purchased five balcony trams from UEC Co in 1907, numbered 46-50. The original print shows the four cylindrical ventilators, and above the lower centre saloon window is the inscription 'Ventilation Patent No 10526'. *E. Hoole*

Above: Birmingham Corporation purchased 150 new top-covered double-deck tramcars during 1906-7. The cars were numbered 71-220 and they were supplied by Dick, Kerr & Co Ltd, who obtained the bodies from the United Electric Car Co Ltd, where car No 163 is seen. *E. Hoole*

Right: Chester Corporation ordered its last five new tramcars in 1907. Numbered 14-8, they were old-fashioned even then, being simple four-wheeled uncanopied open-top double-deck cars. Car No 14 is seen on the 3ft 6in gauge track at Preston. *E. Hoole*

Above: Douglas Corporation in the Isle of Man placed an order with UEC for two cross-bench cable cars for the Upper Douglas Cable Tramway in 1907. Car No 69 is seen being loaded onto the SS *Thursby* at Preston docks. *UEC*

Below: Rotherham Corporation purchased three top-covered double-deck tramcars mounted on UEC Preston compensating four-wheel trucks in 1909. These cars, numbered 32-4, were 20ft long over corner posts and 31ft 6in long overall, and seated 72 passengers. *E. Hoole*

Right: In 1909, the Galway & Salthill Tramway Co purchased five new open-top double-deck horse tramcars. One of these, car No 6, was photographed at Preston. *E. Hoole*

Below: Morecambe Tramway Co ordered its first motorised tramcar in June 1911 and a further two in January 1912. During 1913 a fourth car was supplied, this time an open toastrack. All four had UEC bodies on Leyland chassis. The first three were single-deck petrol-engined tramcars numbered 1-3. Car No 1 is seen when first placed into service during late 1911. *Author's collection*

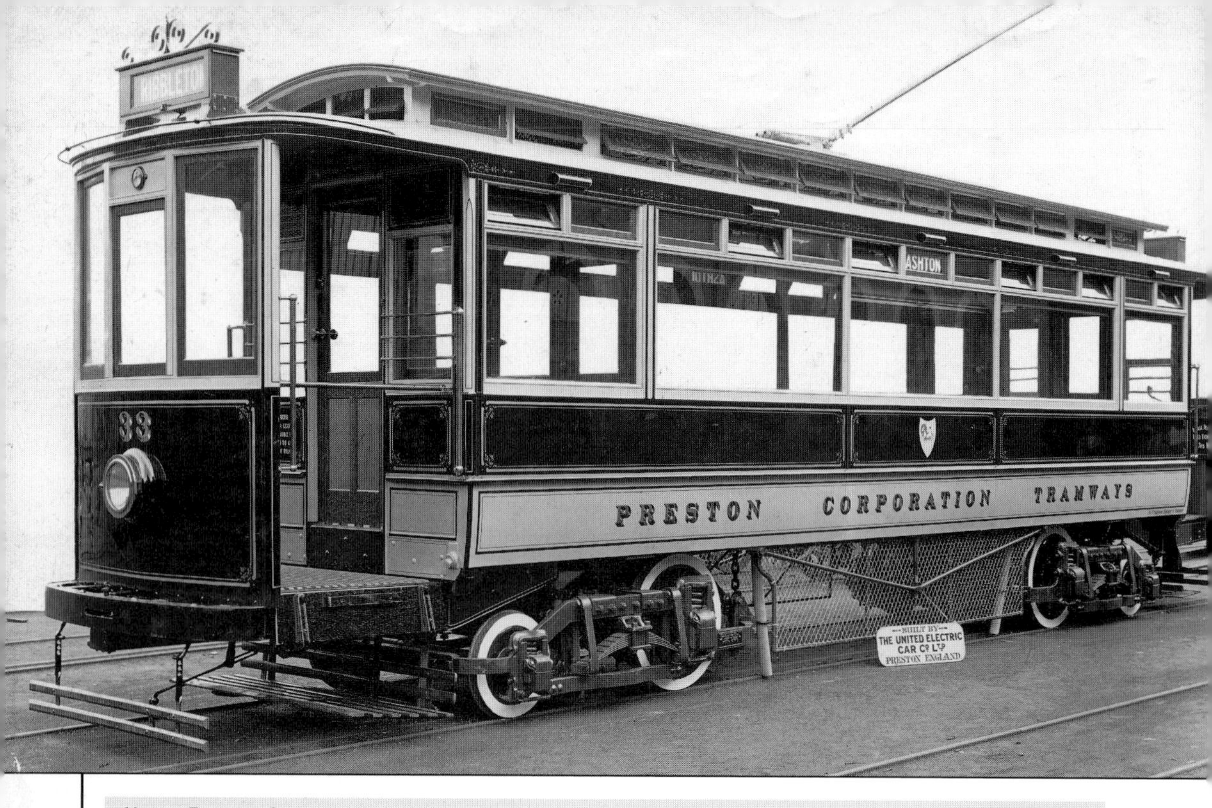

Above: Preston Corporation purchased three single-deck bogie cars from UEC in 1912, of which car No 33 was the last. They seated 44 and were mounted on Brill 39E bogies. *E. Hoole*

Below: In 1912, Balfour Beatty purchased the City of Carlisle Electric Tramways Co Ltd and replaced the original tram fleet with 12 new cars from UEC. These comprised eight open-top double-deck and four single-deck 24-seat tramcars. No 12 is seen at Preston before delivery. *E. Hoole*

Right: This view is of the lower saloon interior of car No 144, one of the 10 balcony cars supplied to Nottingham Corporation by UEC in 1914. The decorations and fittings, which include mirrors in the saloon bulkhead, typify the 'Preston' finish. *E. Hoole*

Below: Oldham Corporation Tramways car No 96 is the subject of this photograph, which was taken around the time World War 1 began. On the back of the print are notes giving delivery dates of November and December 1914, and January 1915. The next photograph of a tramcar for a British customer was of Dunfermline & District Tramways car No 29, built in 1918. *E. Hoole*

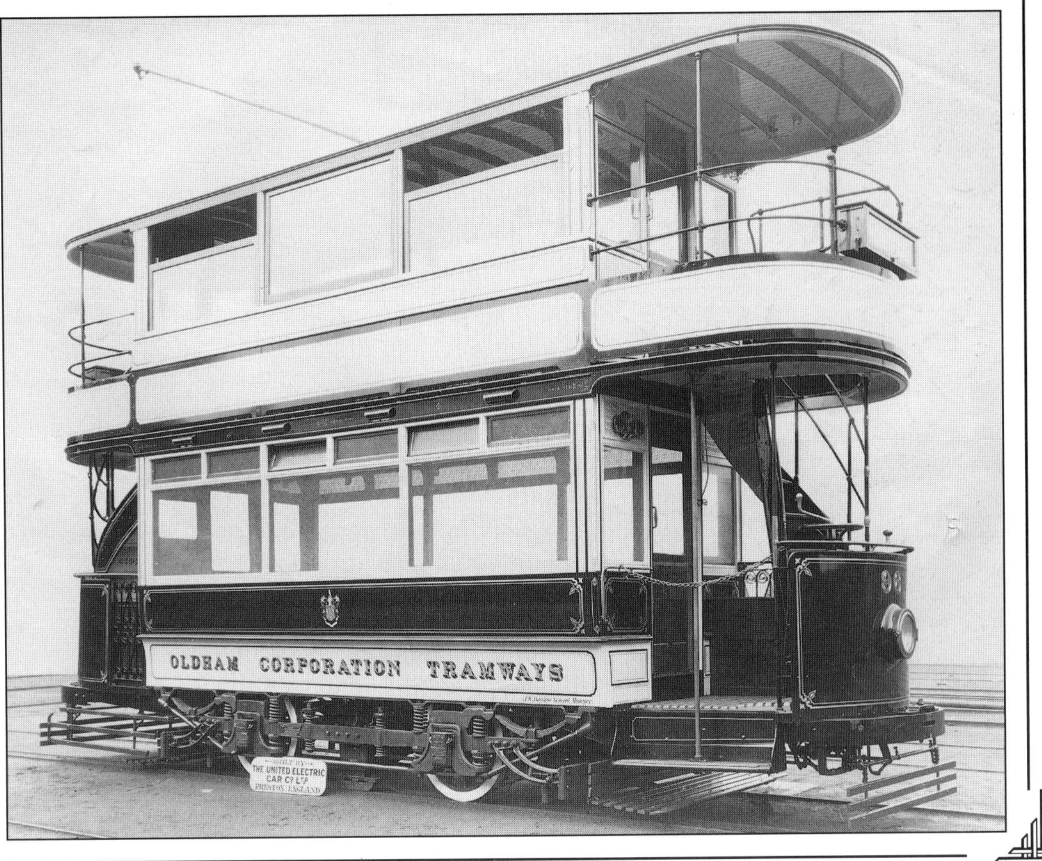

DEWARS THE
NOTTINGHAM CORPORATION

7
ILFORD ROAD
SNEINTON
ONDON ROAD
LLINS
FOOD
BUCHANA
RED
RED SEAL
WHISKY
106
AYS

Previous page: Nottingham Corporation was another municipality to place an order in February 1919, this time for 12 new lower saloon bodies and platforms for existing double-deck cars which Nottingham was rebuilding using existing top decks and trucks. The trucks were re-equipped with new DK30B 40hp motors and new DK DB1 K3 controllers were also provided, whilst the existing upper deck saloon seats were reused. English Electric supplied new seats for the balconies.

During the war, Nottingham had placed a number of similar orders with UEC or DK at Preston for new lower saloon bodies and top covers. However, it is not clear how many were supplied before 1919. The rebuilt cars retained the old car number.

Car No 106 is seen in service in late 1919, and its shabby appearance suggests that it was one of the earliest rebuilds. No 106 was originally built in 1907 with a Milnes Voss body.
Shackleton (Nottingham)

Above: From available records, the first order to be placed with the new English Electric Co Ltd for tramcars was from Morecambe Corporation in 1919 for two horse-drawn toastrack tramcars. These two cars were completed very quickly and entered service before the 1919 holiday season as Nos 14 and 15. *EE*

Right: In 1915, the Balfour Beatty-owned Dunfermline & District Tramways Co promoted an order for the extension of its system to serve the new Royal Naval dockyard at Rosyth. It was urgently required to transport workers to the dock gates from New Row in Dunfermline, where it connected with other tram routes. Unfortunately, the necessary finance and priority certificates were not made available by both the Treasury and the Admiralty until August 1917. The 15 cars were delivered in April 1918. On 17 May 1918, Major Pringle inspected the line for the Board of Trade. The double-track 3ft 6in gauge line was laid on ballast for most of the way and one section was between the two carriageways on the first dual carriageway in Scotland. The Inspector was unhappy with the use of double-deck tramcars on ballasted track, but this was overcome due to the unavailability of single-deck tramcars and pressure from the Admiralty combined with special conditions and restrictions being specified by the Board of Trade to the company in operating the line.

The 15 new open-top cars, Nos 29-43, had been built in Preston by Dick, Kerr & Co Ltd, who had gained full control of UEC Co Ltd in March 1917. They were similar to the previous 28 open-top double-deck cars built by UEC between 1909 and 1912. The cars were 29ft 6in long over fenders, 6ft 2in wide, and the lower saloons were 18ft 2in long over corner pillars. The seating capacity was 55 — 29 on the upper deck and 26 in the lower saloon. The major difference between these cars and those built between 1909-12 was the use of 8ft 0in wheelbase P22 trucks with Peckham Pendulum suspension gear and CJ Spencer slipper brakes which had 2ft 3in-long shoes. The electrical equipment comprised two Dick, Kerr B18 controllers and two General Electric type 249 motors. *DK*

2 Preamble –

Events Leading to the Formation of English Electric

When World War 1 began on 4 August 1914, the British Government quickly imposed restrictions under the Defence of the Realm Act, 1914. In many cases, established engineering companies became Government Controlled Establishments, where the existing equipment and workforce were used to produce materials for the war effort. In Preston, Lancashire, The United Electric Car Co Ltd, the largest of the three remaining electric tramcar manufacturers in Britain, found many of its workforce leaving its employment to join the army.

War work undertaken by the company for the War Department in the period up to the end of June 1915 included 151 pontoon wagons, 72 timber wagons, 2,500 cartridge boxes and 95 pontoons, as well as 60 transport wagon bodies for the Maudsley Motor Company.

During February 1915, the company was involved with both A. V. Roe and the Royal Ordnance Factory, possibly as a subcontractor for aircraft components. In May 1915, the company was in negotiation with the War Department for contracts to machine

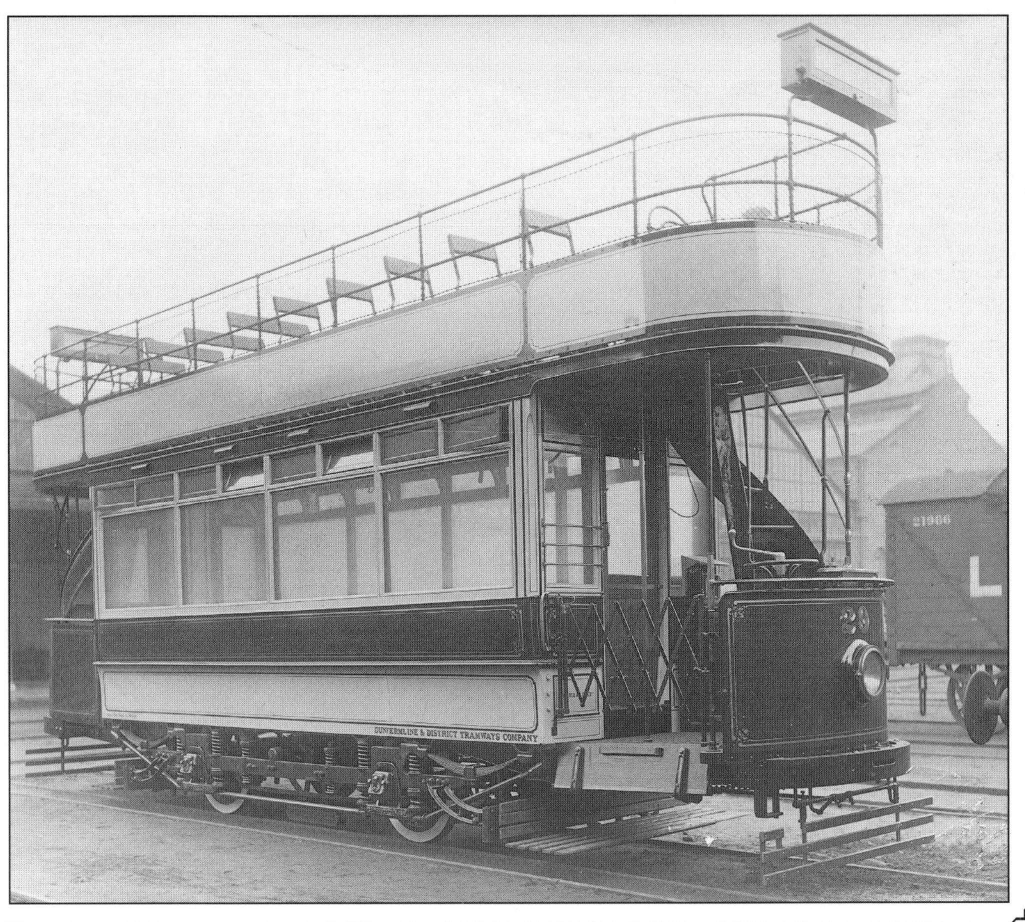

components for 18lb HE shells.

Between 4 August 1914 and 30 June 1915, the company had spent £2,291 13s 4d on purchasing machinery specifically for war work. Some of this equipment — three lathes had been obtained from Leyland Motors Ltd — had been requisitioned by the Government under the Munitions of War Act, 1914. During July 1915, the first contract for the supply of 30,000 shells was received. Over the next 12 months, orders for a total of 400 general service wagons, 500 chassis, 500 cable drums, 400 vehicle props and 75 pontoon boats were fulfilled by the works. By May 1916, 15,211 shells had been supplied, and further extra accommodation was required for war work. The works came under Government control during 1916 following the Munitions of War Act, 1915.

When the company submitted a letter to the Ministry of Munitions in September 1916, it had spent a further £3,406 6s 11d on special machinery for war work in the 12 months to 30 June 1916, and had, at that time, spent nothing on works expansion. A further contract for supplying shells was signed in September 1916, and the supply of shell noses to the Blackburn Munitions Board was undertaken, together with 18lb shrapnel shells. By this time, thousands of shell casings had been rejected by War Office inspectors due to eccentric machining, and these were disposed of as scrap to Hadfields Ltd.

In a report to the Directors in September 1916, it was stated that 184 employees had left the company to join the army. Five of these had been killed or were missing, three were prisoners of war and five had been wounded in action. Tramcar production had taken a back seat, but between May and December 1916 the following orders were recorded in the surviving company records, (*below*):

May 1916	Top covers for SLT at £123 4s 0d each, ref F9336
July 1916	One top-covered car for Sunderland six car bodies for Nottingham
August 1916	Four top-covered car bodies via BTH for Mansfield
November 1916	Six car bodies and two top covers for Nottingham, and two car bodies for Rotherham
December 1916	Five skeleton car bodies for SLT at £125 0s 0d each, ref F9707

Below left: Another Lancashire seaside resort, this time Southport, was also quick off the mark to order three new open toastrack tramcar bodies for mounting on to existing trucks which the Corporation had salvaged from earlier single-deck cars. The three bodies, Nos 29, 31 and 33, were ordered on 6 February 1919, with delivery promised between April and June 1919, again just in time for the holiday season. Car No 31 is seen waiting for passengers outside the Monument, Lord Street, before departing on the circular tour of the town. *courtesy A. D. Packer collection*

Above: At the beginning of March 1919, Liverpool Corporation was desperate for new tramcars to improve the fleet, a quarter of which was waiting for repairs due to wartime neglect. An order was placed for 25 new cars to be completed at the rate of three per week from July 1919. These cars followed traditional prewar tramcar designs, being 28ft long, 6ft 9in wide and mounted on 7ft 6in wheelbase Preston 21E trucks. The electrical equipment comprised two DK20 A SPL 40hp motors and DK DB1 K3 controllers. Seating for 64 passengers was provided — 22 on longitudinal seats in the lower saloon and 36 on double seats in the upper saloon, with the remaining six being accommodated on a curved seat for three on each balcony.

The cars, numbered 609-33, were delivered by road for final assembly and testing at Liverpool's Lambeth Road works, with the first 22 entering service during late 1919. *Richard Brown (Liverpool)*

These cars could be produced by UEC only if the customer was able to provide a Priority 'A' certificate from the Ministry of Munitions. As SLT was producing shells in the company's workshops at Atherton, and the Sunderland car was a replacement for one destroyed by the enemy, there was no problem with these. The Mansfield order was also completed, but the author has yet to find confirmation that the car bodies for Nottingham were built. Rotherham, unable to obtain a certificate, purchased 10 secondhand tramcars from London County Council.

In January 1917, the various subsidiary companies of the United Electric Car Co Ltd were all wound up voluntarily, with any remaining assets being transferred to UEC. These included Electric Railway & Tramway Carriage Works Ltd, G. F. Milnes & Co Ltd and British Electric Car Co Ltd. In March 1917, Dick, Kerr and Co Ltd, who had a financial interest and had been represented on the UEC board since it was formed in 1905, gained full control of the company after exchanging shares.

Dick, Kerr & Co Ltd had owned the West Works on the opposite side of Strand Road from the car works since 1903. The two companies had worked together for many years and with both factories under Government control, it was advantageous to combine their activities under the control of a single management.

The Dick, Kerr Works had originally been built to provide electrical equipment for electric traction purposes. It had also become a Government Controlled Establishment for special war work and was producing substantial quantities of shells and other armaments, and these works had been expanded by 25% to cope with demand. Details of much of the works' output is not known, but in November 1916, Dick, Kerr & Co Ltd and British Westinghouse Ltd both received orders from the Railway Operating Division of the Royal Engineers for 100 petrol-electric two-axle locomotives for the 60cm gauge lines used to carry ammunition to the front lines in France. The Dick, Kerr locomotives had Dorman petrol engines, Phoenix generators and Dick, Kerr electric motors and gearboxes. In 1917, aircraft production was added to the many activities being undertaken in both East and West Works at Preston.

Since all this war work meant close co-operation with other companies involved in producing castings or components needed at Preston, in 1917, Dick, Kerr & Co Ltd acquired control of Willans & Robinson Ltd, whose plant included a large foundry. At this point in June 1917, the capital issued for the expanded company was £650,000. Contracts for 100 aircraft were placed with Dick, Kerr & Co Ltd at Preston in March 1918. These were for type F3 flying boats.

The war ended on 11 November 1918, and on 21 November 1918 the Government passed the Ministry of Munitions Act, 1918 allowing the 'Ministry of Munitions to supervise and regulate the diversion to the

Below: Bradford Corporation was another municipality to place an order in early March 1919 for 26 new tramcars. These were 4ft 0in gauge Preston 21E 7ft 0in wheelbase trucks fitted with two DK31B 45hp motors. Seating for 65 passengers was provided, 22 in the lower saloon and 43 on top. The 26 cars were numbered 233-58 and delivery commenced during late 1919, with 16 cars entering service before the beginning of 1920. *EE*

production of articles required in times of peace, of industries established or utilised during the present war for the production of war material'. Quick off the mark to exploit the potential worldwide market in the development of the use of electric power, a group of people from the John Brown group of companies incorporated and registered a new company on 14 December 1918. This new company, The English Electric Co Ltd, was registered as a private company with a capital of £5,000,000 to consolidate and co-ordinate under one control the following companies:

1. The Coventry Ordnance Works Ltd
2. The Phoenix Dynamo Manufacturing Co Ltd
3a. Dick, Kerr & Co Ltd
b. The United Electric Car Co Ltd
c. Willans & Robinson Ltd

The first directors (listed below) were representative of major engineering and shipbuilding interests. Four of these were also directors of major English railway companies, and it was predicted that these connections

Below: In April 1916, Huddersfield Corporation placed an order with UEC Co Ltd for the supply of six tramcars to cope with the increased traffic generated by the various factories engaged on war work in the town. In February 1919, Huddersfield, which had failed to get priority certificates for these six, increased the order to 20.

The first six cars, Nos 107-12, were delivered during the autumn of 1919, with the additional 14 cars, Nos 113-26, arriving between March and October 1920. The two batches had minor differences, reflecting the availability of materials at the time of construction. The car bodies were 7ft 0in wide and 16ft 0in long with an overall car length of 29ft 0in, and were mounted on 7ft 6in wheelbase Preston 21E trucks. The electrical equipment comprised two 40hp DK30B motors and DK DB1-K3B controllers. Seating was provided for 22 in the lower saloon and 40 in the upper saloon and balconies. The trucks were supplied suitable for a wheel gauge of 4ft $7\frac{9}{16}$in to suit Huddersfield's track gauge of 4ft $7\frac{3}{4}$in.

Car No 113 was photographed outside Huddersfield's Great Northern Street works on 10 March 1920.
Courtesy Roy Brook collection

SPECIAL CAR
LONGSIGHT, ARDWICK & MARKET St.
800
CLAYTON & OLD TRAFFORD via PICCADILLY
27·G
835

Left: In March 1919, Manchester Corporation placed an order for 50 tram bodies; 38 were to be high capacity totally enclosed double bogie cars of an up-to-date design, with the other 12 being single-deck combination cars built to a specification which was archaic by 1919.

The 35ft 0in-long double-deck car bodies were mounted on Brush type 22E 4ft 0in wheelbase bogies. Seating for 78 passengers was provided, with 32 in the lower and 46 in the upper saloons respectively. The car bodies were dispatched by rail to Manchester for final assembly.

Delivery commenced in late 1919, with the first cars being placed into service during December 1919 and the last in December 1920. The batch was numbered 798-835.

Car No 800 is seen posing for the official photographer in January 1920. It is parked on the sidings at Heaton Park, Manchester, which now forms part of the preserved tramway operated by the Manchester Tramway Museum Society. *EE*

Below left: Numerically, the last car to be delivered, car No 835, is seen in Devonshire Street North outside Hyde Road depot in December 1920. *EE*

would materially support the company with orders.

* Chairman: Sir Charles Edward Ellis GBE, KCB, Managing Director, John Brown & Co Ltd; Director, The Great Eastern Railway Co.

* Joint Managing Directors: Lt-Col Sir John Herbert Mansell KBE, Managing Director, The Coventry Ordnance Works Ltd; Percy J. Pybus CBE, Managing Director, Phoenix Dynamo Manufacturing Co Ltd; Walter Rutherford,Managing Director, Dick, Kerr & Co Ltd.

Below: The 12 single-deck combination cars were placed into service on Manchester's only single-deck tram route No 53 during December 1920 and January 1921. These cars were 36ft 6in long and had identical bogies and electrical equipment to the 38 double-deck cars. The cars seated 28 in the saloon and six on each of the two open-sided cross-bench sections and were numbered 836-47.

One of these cars poses outside the Devonshire Street North entrance to Hyde Road depot in December 1920. *EE*

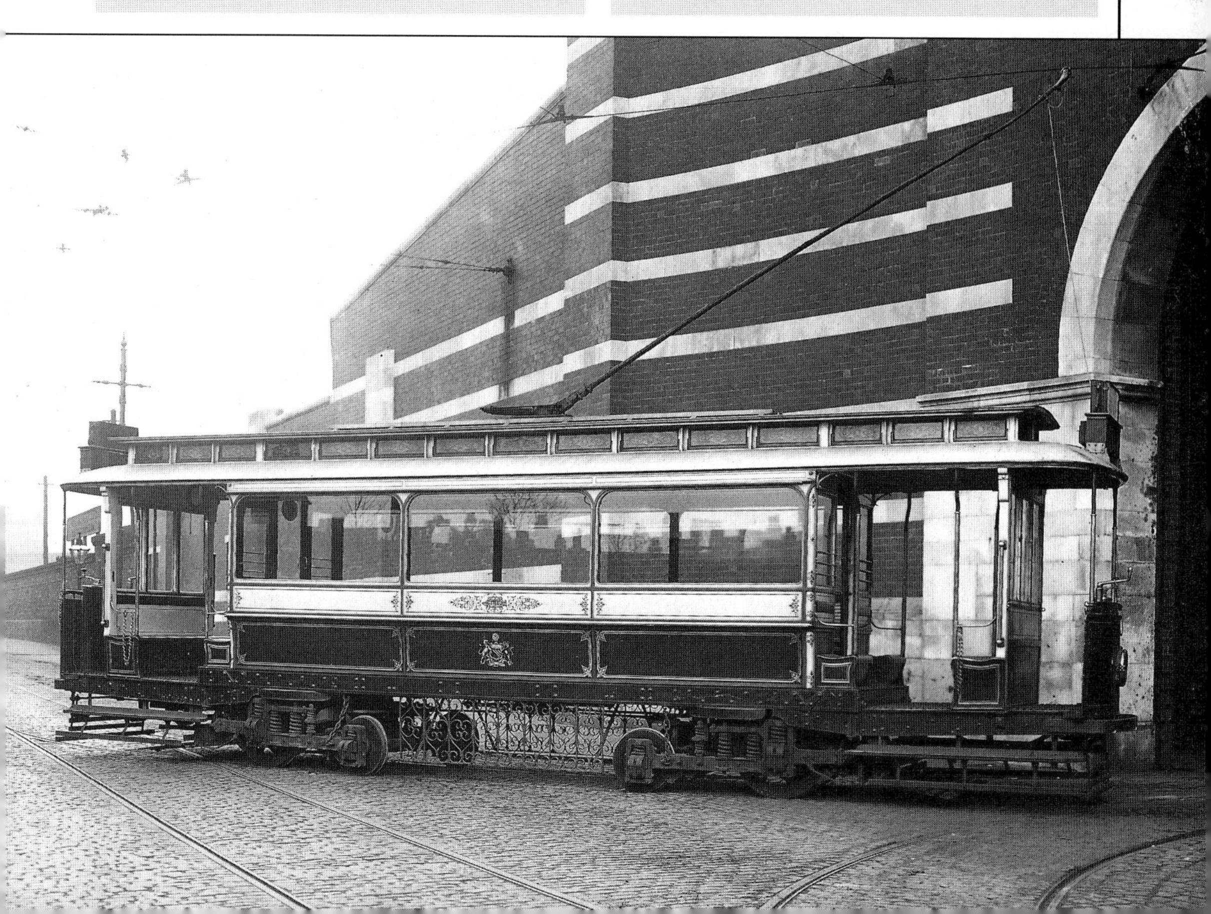

Above: In 1918, Burton upon Trent Corporation had to hire eight tramcars from Great Yarmouth Corporation for use on the Branston Road route to carry workers to a new factory built to manufacture machine guns.

They were hired for six months, commencing in September 1918. With the end of the war in November 1918 and the rundown of the munitions industry, Burton still found it necessary to order four new vestibuled top-covered balcony cars from Preston in early March 1919. These 3ft 6in gauge cars, numbered 21-4, arrived in early 1920 and were mounted on 6ft 0in wheelbase Preston trucks. The electrical equipment fitted comprised two 30hp DK29A motors and DK DB1-K3 controllers. Seating was provided for a total of 46 passengers.

In 1930, these four cars were resold to York Corporation, who converted them to open-top cars. This photograph shows car No 22, which incidentally overturned in November 1921 after suffering a broken axle.
Courtesy Roy Marshall collection

* Directors: Sir John A. F. Aspinall MInst C E, Director, Lancashire & Yorkshire Railway Co; Claud T. Cayley, Chairman, Dick, Kerr & Co Ltd; Bernard A. Firth, Chairman, Thomas Firth & Sons Ltd, Director, Great Northern Railway Co; Sir Alexander Gracie KBE, MVO, Chairman, The Fairfield Shipbuilding & Engineering Co Ltd; William Lionel Hitchens, Chairman, Cammell, Laird & Co Ltd, Director, London & North Western Railway Co; John Sampson CBE, Director, John Brown & Co Ltd, Director, Harland & Wolff.

The new company quickly acquired the share capital of both private companies — Coventry Ordnance and Phoenix Dynamo. Before the end of 1918, Dick, Kerr sent a letter to its shareholders recommending them to accept the offer to exchange shares on terms which were attractive. The shareholders were told:

'Your directors believe that the future success of electrical companies will depend upon their capacity to undertake and carry out large schemes such as the electrification of railways, the construction of large central power stations and the development of hydro-electric installations. As you will see from the enclosed particulars, the new company's Board is a strong one, and the three companies concerned in the proposed amalgamation will be in a position to undertake and carry to completion schemes of the greatest magnitude. We are satisfied that the position of each of the companies concerned will be greatly strengthened by combination with the others. The directors, therefore, strongly recommend the shareholders to accept the offer which is now made. Your directors intend to exchange their shares on the terms offered and they have ascertained that the holders of a large part of the share capital will also accept these terms.'

The new company made Queen's House in Kingsway, London WC2, its headquarters and the prospectus for debentures was issued by the company on 12 July 1919. In this, it was stated that the company owned 95% of the Dick, Kerr shares and that so far, 419,131 Preference £1 shares and 1,418,629 Ordinary £1 shares had been issued, out of the authorised 1,500,000 6% cumulative Preference shares and 3,500,000 Ordinary shares.

By this time, the several works had been converted back from conditions of munition manufacture and other war work, and each was to specilise in the type of work best suited to its equipment, much of which had been installed for war work. In the first six months from Armistice Day, the group had taken orders to the value of £1,500,000, but the delay in conversion meant that other orders had been lost due to customers being unable to wait.

In November 1919, English Electric Co Ltd bought the Siemens Dynamo Works at Stafford from the Custodian of Enemy Property. In December 1919, English Electric, which had

Below: Another customer for new tramcars was Doncaster Corporation, which in March 1919 ordered 10 top-covered vestibuled cars mounted on Peckham Pendulum P22 7ft 6in wheelbase trucks. The electrical equipment was two 40hp DK30B motors and DK DB1 K3 controllers.

Seating was provided for 66 passengers, 26 in the lower and 40 in the upper saloons. They were delivered in late 1919, as Fleet Nos 38-47, and were the last tramcars to be purchased by Doncaster, which introduced trolleybus replacements progressively from August 1928.

Car No 46 is seen on Frenchgate with the Corporation's Greyfriars Road power station in the background in late 1919. *EE*

already absorbed the manufacturing interests of Dick, Kerr & Co Ltd, acquired a holding of ordinary shares in a new company formed by J. G. White & Co Ltd called the Consolidated Construction Co, to amalgamate the contracting business of Dick, Kerr & Co Ltd and J. G. White & Co Ltd. The new company, English Electric Co Ltd, was now poised to become one of the three giants involved in the electrical industry.

At this point, it is convenient to leave the development of the group and concentrate on the tramcar manufacturing side of the business, which continued in the former United Electric Car works on the East side of Strand Road. These works comprised just 5.7% of the total assets of the new company and were responsible for 4% of the total liabilities in 1918. Following the purchase of Siemens, this proportion fell further.

The author hopes that this preamble puts into perspective how small the tramcar and bodybuilding contribution actually was within the group's turnover.

Below: Like many other systems after the war, Nottingham Corporation was faced with a backlog of repair work. In addition to the ongoing repair and rebuilding programme for most of the existing fleet, an order was placed in April 1919 for 25 new 58-seat cars from English Electric. Numbered 156-80, they were expected to be delivered at the rate of two per month from December 1919. However, due to problems with suppliers of brake components, the first delivery was not made until May 1920 when 10 cars arrived in Nottingham without the Peacock brake gear, and it was some time before the strike at the brake manufacturers was resolved.

The cars were fitted with vestibuled platforms, and car No 164 is seen in 1934.
S. J. Eades, courtesy G. H. F. Atkins collection

Right: The City of Lincoln Tramways, one of Britain's smallest systems with only 1.84 route miles of track, was operated from 1905-19 by eight tramcars which obtained current from the 'Griffiths-Bedell' surface contact system. Studs were placed at 8ft 0in intervals in the centre of the track. In 1919, the system was changed to overhead wire collection, and three additional unvestibuled top-covered double-deck cars, numbered 9-11, were purchased from English Electric. By the time Lincoln closed its system in March 1929, the platforms had been vestibuled, and the cars were then sold to Preston Corporation for further use.

Lincoln No 11 became Preston No 22, and is seen loading in 1931 for the Circular service route F to Fulwood via North Road and Withy Trees. *M. J. O'Connor, courtesy F. P. Groves*

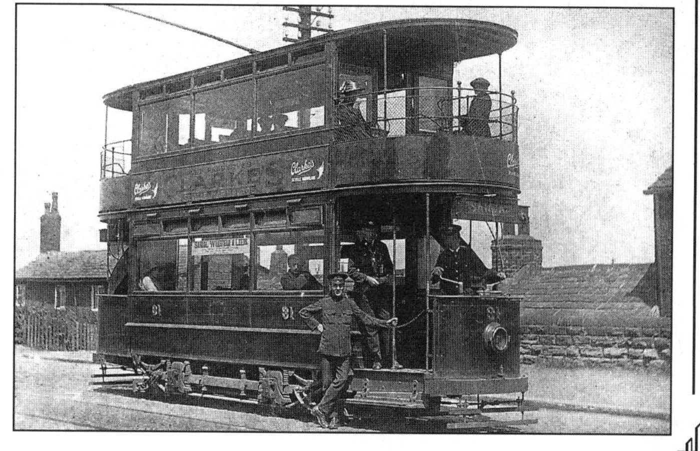

Below right: A serious fire in March 1917 destroyed eight of the 16 tramcars housed in the Castleford depot of the Yorkshire (West Riding) Electric Tramways Co Ltd. Eight cars were transferred from Wakefield to maintain services on the isolated Castleford system. In May 1919, eight new tramcars were ordered from Preston as replacements and were given the fleet numbers of those lost in the fire.

The cars were 28ft 0in long, 7ft 1in wide and were mounted on 7ft 6in wheelbase Preston four-wheel trucks. The electrical equipment comprised two 40hp DK20A2 motors and DK DB1-K4 controllers. The cars entered service at Wakefield in 1920, and car No 31 is seen *en route* to Sandal. *Courtesy Roy Brook collection*

Below: In May 1919, Wigan Corporation ordered six tramcars to a very similar specification to the West Riding ones, the main difference being the use of 40hp DK30B motors. The cars were numbered 7-12, and despite asking for an August 1919 delivery date, Wigan did not receive them until early January 1920, and even had to accept three of them unpainted.

The first car was placed into service in February 1920. These cars cost £2,025 each and were fitted with C. J. Spencer mechanical slipper brakes. Interestingly, a further six identical cars were supplied to Wigan between June 1921 and April 1922, but this time they carried bodies built in Wigan by Massey Bros and they had been ordered in March 1920. What is still unknown is how or why Massey had the EE body drawings.

Car No 9 is seen in Wigan town centre in the late 1920s.
Leyland Motors, courtesy R. Marshall collection

Above right: At the end of the war, Rotherham Corporation Tramways, previously unsuccessful in its 1916 application for Ministry of Munitions priority certificates for two bodies to replace damaged trams, invited tenders for various complete trams and car bodies. In May 1919, three orders were placed with the Preston Works. The first was for four complete top-covered double-deck cars mounted on 7ft 6in wheelbase Preston four-wheel trucks fitted with C. J. Spencer slipper brakes, two 40hp DK30 motors and DB1-K3 controllers. The bodies cost £2,190 with promised delivery quoted as 24 weeks. These four cars were delivered in April-May 1920.

Our photograph shows car No 11 photographed at Preston before delivery and fitting of the trolley pole and C. J. Spencer slipper brakes. These four cars are believed to have been renumbered 1-4 by Rotherham shortly after delivery. *EE*

Below right: The other orders placed were for 11 new standard bodies complete with top-deck narrow-slat garden seats. Rotherham was to supply the trucks and fit top covers when delivered from earlier tramcars which needed major overhauls. In early November 1919, the order was reduced from 11 to seven. The final order was for the supply of an especially long body, again with Rotherham supplying the truck and the top cover from one of the three 1903 single-deck ER&TCW-built tramcars, which had been converted to double-deck trams in 1908 utilising new UEC top covers.

These eight bodies were delivered six months late during the summer of 1920, and the quoted price was £1,705 each.

Rotherham No 8 is seen in Frederick Street, Rotherham, shortly before the Canklow tram service was withdrawn on 9 July 1934.
M. J. O'Connor, courtesy A. D. Packer

DEPOT ONLY
CANKLOW
WHITWORTHS
WATH ALES
HUDSONS
SAFETY
FIRST
SURELY
MEANS
BOVRIL
DAVIES & JOHNSON
HOUSE FURNISHERS

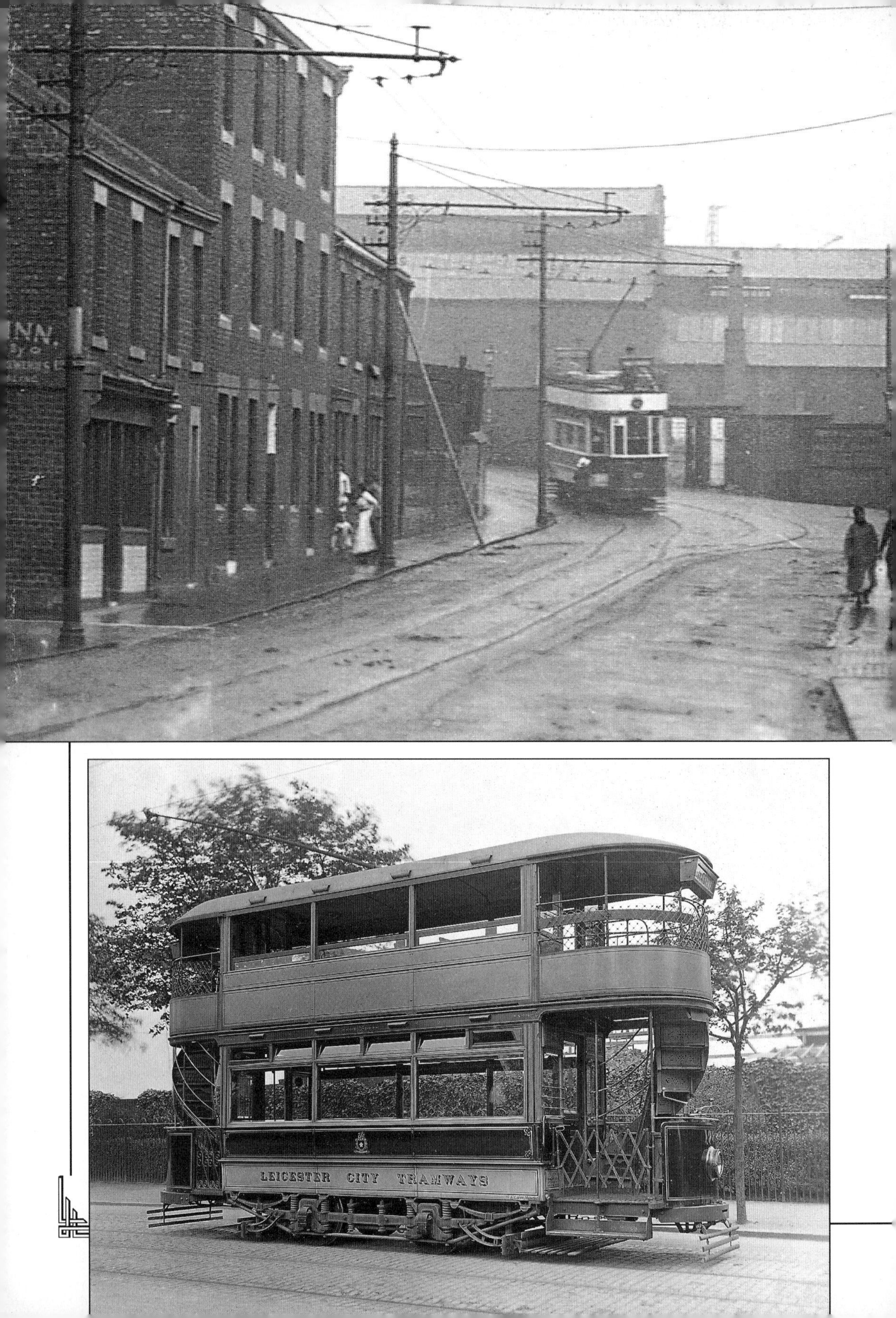
LEICESTER CITY TRAMWAYS

Left: In May 1919, the Tyneside Tramways & Tramroads Co ordered three open-top double-deck cars mounted on 7ft 6in wheelbase Preston 21E trucks. The cars were fitted with platform vestibules and seated 59, 22 in the lower saloon. The electrical equipment comprised two DK30B 40hp motors and DB1-K3 controllers.

The cars were numbered 28-30, but before delivery commenced, Tyneside Tramways & Tramroads Co placed a further order in October 1919 for another open-top double-deck car body which was to be mounted on to an existing truck salvaged from works car No 27 to form the new car 27 in 1920.

Car No 27 is seen in Stephenson Street, Howdon. *Roy Brook collection*

Below left: In June 1919, Leicester Corporation chose to purchase 12 tramcars practically identical to the ones it had bought in 1905 from UEC at Preston. The resulting cars, given fleet numbers 167-78, had more powerful motors, being two 40hp DK25A against the 35hp DK3A4 on the earlier cars. Unusually for 1920-built cars, they had reversed staircases.

Car No 178 is seen in Abbey Park Road close to the Corporation's tramway workshops and depot. *Burton (Leicester)*

Below: Southampton Corporation was also another customer which purchased a standard Preston open-vestibule, open-balcony car. Its order for 10 was placed in June 1919, and delivery was completed in early 1920, with the cars being numbered 82-91.

Car No 83 is seen in Southampton a few months after entering service. *EE*

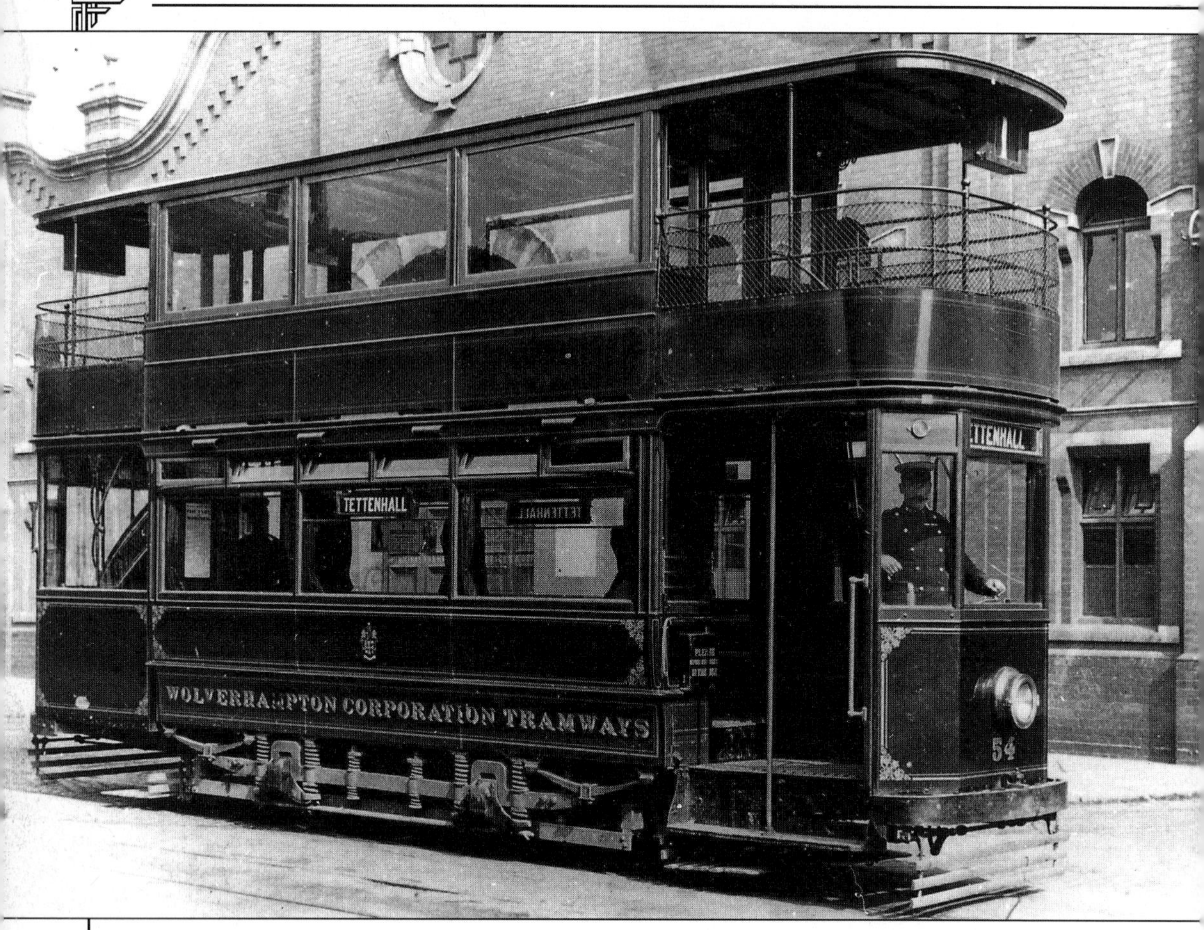

Above: Wolverhampton Corporation ordered six tramcar bodies from English Electric in June 1919. Four of these were open-balcony vestibuled double-deck cars, car Nos 53-6, and the other two cars, Nos 57 and 58, were single-deck combination cars for use on the routes with low bridges.

The double-deck cars seated 53, 22 in the lower saloon and 31 on the upper deck. The cars, as delivered in September 1920, were fitted for use on the 'Lorain' surface-contact system in which the current was collected from studs in the centre of the tram track. During the early 1920s, Wolverhampton converted all of its routes to overhead wire supply.
Wolverhampton Corporation, courtesy Roy Marshall collection

Left: No photographs of Wolverhampton's single-deck combination cars Nos 57-8 in service have been found. Instead it has therefore been necessary to include this 1950 view of one of these two cars which had become a store shed near Dudley after being withdrawn from service.
NTM collection

Right: When South Shields Corporation obtained powers in 1921 to extend its system to serve the new housing estates being built at Cleadon, it had already placed an order with English Electric for the supply of five double-deck totally enclosed bogie cars. Capable of carrying 82 seated passengers, they were to incorporate a front exit system utilising the Hatton straight staircase. The cars, costing £3,300 each, were 34ft 6in long, 7ft 2in wide and weighed 16 tons. The bodies were mounted on Brill 76E equal wheel bogies with 32in diameter wheels. The electrical equipment comprised two 50hp DK type 31A motors, with EE DB1 form K4C controllers.

The five cars, numbered 41-5, were delivered in early 1921, and car No 44 is seen at the Cleadon Ridgeway terminus. *Courtesy D. Harvey*

Below right: Since 1900, Oldham Corporation had been one of the regular purchasers of Preston-built tramcars, and it ordered a further 12 in August 1919. They were to be the same as the 11 supplied in 1915. The cars had open-ended balconies and seated 58, with the usual 22 on longitudinal seats in the lower saloon. The 7ft 0in wheelbase trucks were fitted with two 40hp DK30B motors and EE DB1 K3 controllers completed the electrical equipment. The cars carried Fleet Nos 4-12 and 14-6, and entered service in 1921.

Car No 12 is seen in Oldham town centre *en route* to Waterhead from Hollinwood. *A. D. Packer*

Above: The small, Corporation-owned 3ft 6in gauge tramway system in the Kent town of Dover ordered three open-top tramcars from EE in July 1919. These 58 seat cars, with 22 seats in the lower saloon, were mounted on Preston 7ft 6in wheelbase trucks. The electrical equipment comprised two 40hp DK30B motors and EE type DB1-K3 controllers. They were delivered in 1920 and were numbered 25-7 by the Corporation. In 1928, they were fitted with top covers purchased from Birmingham & Midland Tramways.

Car No 27 is seen passing a Southern Railway P-type tank locomotive in Strond Street, Dover in July 1934. *G. N. Southerden*

Right: In September 1919, Stockport Corporation ordered 10 totally enclosed double-deck car bodies from English Electric for mounting on 7ft 0in wheelbase Peckham Pendulum trucks supplied by Brush Electrical Engineering Co Ltd. The trucks were fitted with two 40hp DK30B motors and EE type DB1-K3B controllers.

These cars had folding platform doors when delivered between late 1920 and early 1921, and carried Fleet Nos 51-60. Car No 54 is seen outside the depot and carries paper adverts for the new films *Hobson's Choice* and *The Miracle Man* at the town's cinemas. *EE*

Above right: Swindon Corporation operated a small 3ft 6in gauge tramway system serving three routes radiating from the Great Western Railway station. The 12-car fleet was strengthened by the purchase of one English Electric-built car in 1920. The vestibuled open-top double-deck car No 13, seating 54, was mounted on a 6ft 6in wheelbase Preston truck, and the electrical equipment comprised two 30hp DK29A motors and EE type DB1-K4 controllers.

After the system closed in July 1929, the body was sold to become a garden shed in Chisledon. It has since been rescued for a preservation project. *A. D. Packer*

STOCKPORT CORPORATION TRAMWAYS

Left: In September 1919, Sunderland Corporation decided to purchase six totally enclosed double-deck tramcars mounted on new Peckham Pendulum 8ft 6in wheelbase trucks. They cost £1,902 each, and Sunderland was to use old DK25A motors and DE1-A controllers taken from earlier cars. The 58-seat bodies were to be fitted with the Hatton straight staircase and front exit doors.

A few months after placing this order, Sunderland decided to purchase a further six tramcars to the same design. However, these cars carried new electrical equipment comprising two 30hp DK29A motors and DB1-K4 controllers. Delivery of the cars, numbered 72-7 and 78-83 respectively, began in May 1921. The cars were sent by rail for reassembly in Sunderland, and they progressively entered service over the next six months.

Car No 72 is seen at the Sea Lane terminus at Seaburn when new. Unusually, the side destination box states Seaside Lane, and the car is fitted with the traditional trolley boom.
EE print

Centre left: In 1931, Sunderland changed over to the Bow Collector system, and car No 78 had been rebuilt as a conventional type car by removing the front exit, and the straight 'Hatton' staircases were also replaced by standard Sunderland 90° direct spiral stairs.
Sunderland Corporation/Author's collection

Below left: Bolton Corporation was another customer to purchase eight new trams to the same specification as its prewar trams. These unvestibuled, open balcony, top-covered bogie cars, mounted on Brill 22E maximum traction bogie trucks, were fitted with two 40hp DK9A motors. The 74-seat cars, numbered 113-20, were supplied in 1921 and were fitted with longitudinal seats for 30 in the lower saloon.

An unidentified car from this batch is seen inside Bradshawgate Depot.
EE

Right: Stockport Corporation, having placed an order for 10 new tramcars with English Electric, realised that the delivery promised for these was not going to help the chronic shortage of serviceable cars. In September 1919, it approached English Electric at Preston for help. EE offered to supply a number of standard open-top car bodies from stock. If Stockport salvaged top covers and trucks from existing cars awaiting repair, it could solve the crisis. Costing £860 each, five lower saloon body assemblies were purchased, and these were delivered in October 1919. Whilst the interiors of the saloons were finished, the outsides were still in grey primer. The first two cars were completed and had entered service by December 1919, the others following in early 1920. All five ran with grey outsides until sufficient cars were serviceable to allow them to be finished. They were all fitted with vestibules in 1929-30. In February 1944, cars Nos 61-5 were renumbered 6, 9, 11, 29 and 10 respectively to allow all low-bridge cars to be numbered in the group 1-29.

Car No 10 (ex-65) is seen on 27 May 1947 in Mersey Square, Stockport. *A. D. Packer*

Centre right: Portsmouth Corporation Tramways' General Manager, Mr W. R. Spaven, anxious to improve the quality of the fleet under his control, specified fully enclosed tramcars when the Corporation placed an order with EE in October 1919 for 12 new cars costing £1,930 each. These cars were delivered by rail in sections to Cosham railway station between 5 October and 11 November 1920. They were assembled quickly and placed into service, complete with curtains for the lower saloon windows! The cars were numbered 105-16 and had 6ft 0in wheelbase Preston four-wheel trucks fitted with two DK20 A2 motors. The 58-seat bodies had the usual 22 longitudinal seats in the lower saloon.

Car No 107 is seen at South Parade Pier. *A. D. Packer collection*

Below right: Darwen Corporation was another customer to place a repeat order with Preston for another three open-top bogie cars, duplicates of ones supplied by UEC in 1915. However, this time, the new 66-seat cars — 30 in the lower saloon — had EE Burnley-type maximum traction bogies fitted with EE 40hp DK20A2 motors. The cars were numbered 20-2.

Car No 22 is seen in open country shortly after delivery in 1921, and the EE print, No P3000, was the first of a new series of photographs identified by prefix P for Preston. *EE*

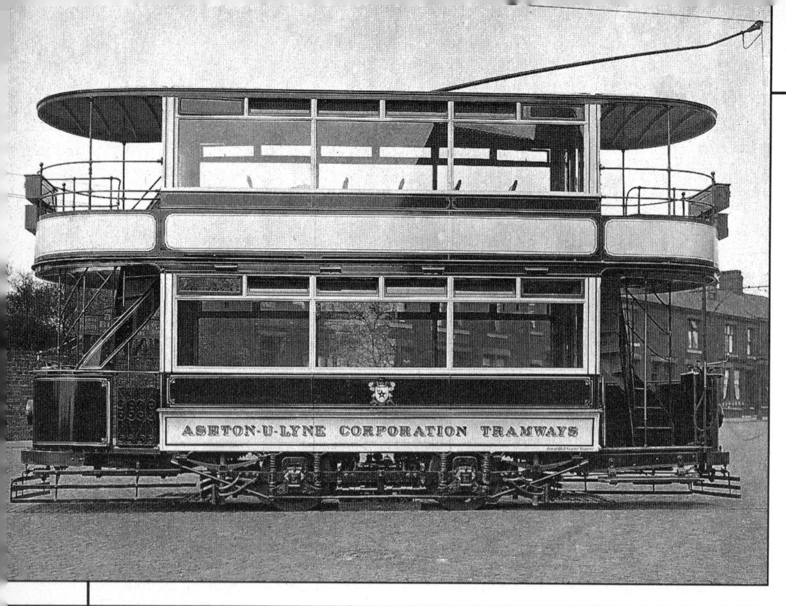

Left: Ashton-under-Lyne Corporation obtained sanction from the Board of Trade to borrow £25,000 to cover the cost of purchasing 12 new top-covered double-deck unvestibuled tramcars from English Electric. They were mounted on 6ft 6in wheelbase Brill 21E trucks fitted with C. H. Spencer 'Huddersfield' type slipper brakes. The electrical equipment comprised two 40hp DK 30B1 motors and EE DB1-K3 controllers. The cars, numbered 27-38, were delivered in early 1921, and one of the cars is shown fitted outside the Mossley Road Depot. *EE*

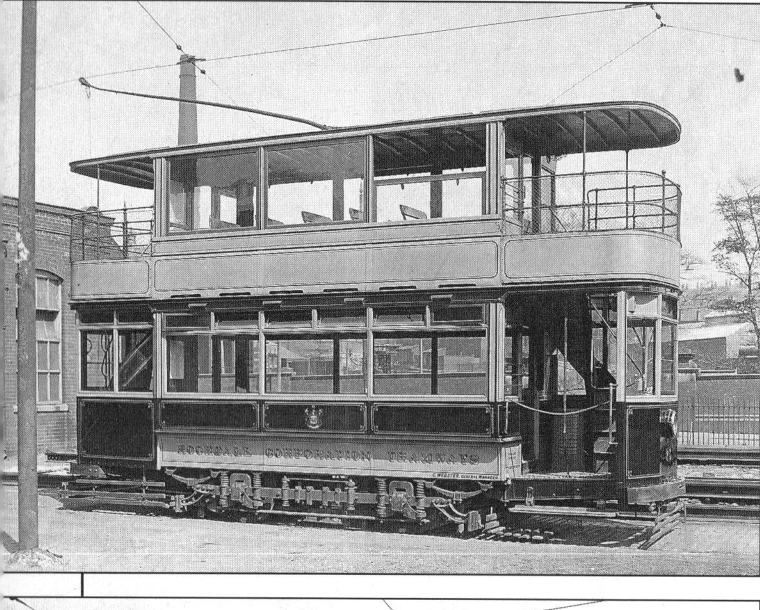

Centre left: Rochdale Corporation was the last customer to place an order in 1919 for new tramcars, this time specifying 58-seat top-covered double-deck cars with vestibuled platforms and open-ended balconies. The cars were mounted on 7ft 6in wheelbase Brill 21E trucks, and the electrical equipment comprised two 40hp DK30B motors and EE DB1-K3B controllers. Numbered 70-9, the cars arrived in late 1920.

Car No 75 is seen in Mellor Street depot yard. *EE*

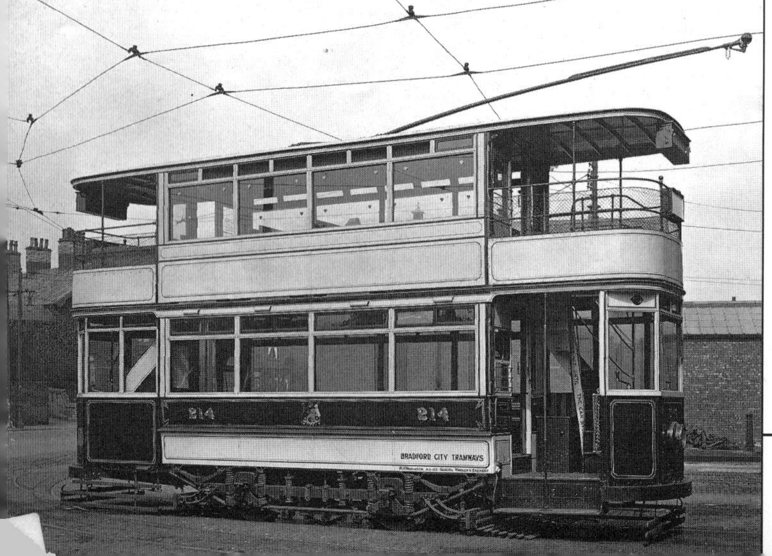

Below left: Early 1920 saw Bradford Corporation ordering a batch of 20 trams, almost identical to cars currently being delivered by English Electric. Normal type rails around the balconies were specified for these trams, which were to receive Fleet Nos 213-32, whereas the earlier batch had been fitted with the deep tin type. Car No 214 is seen outside Thornbury depot. *EE*

Above: Manchester Corporation was another customer to re-order a further batch of cars once delivery had started of its earlier order. This time, a further 50 double-deck bogie cars with vestibules were ordered in late 1919. Delivery of these cars, numbered 848-97, began in April 1921 and continued to September 1921. However, due to the economic slump, deliveries did not recommence until February 1922, the order being completed in August 1922.

One of these cars, No 896, is seen in 1938 at Hazel Grove, Stockport.
W. A. Camwell, courtesy F. P. Groves

Below: Colne Corporation ordered two large 68-seat vestibuled balcony double-deck bogie cars from English Electric in January 1920. The cars were mounted on 4ft 0in wheelbase Burnley maximum traction bogies, and were built to negotiate a bridge near Colne station with a headroom of 15ft 7in. *Dr Hugh Nicol*

Above: Balfour Beatty & Co placed an order with EE in February 1920 for the supply of four 3ft 6in gauge double-deck cars with open tops and platform vestibules. The trucks were 8ft 0in wheelbase Preston type 21E with Peckham Pendulum Gear. They were for the Cheltenham & District Light Railway Co. The electric equipment comprised 2-MV type 323 35hp motors and Westinghouse T1/C controllers.

The cars, numbered 21-4, were completed at Preston, when Balfour Beatty arranged for car No 24 to be diverted in August 1921 to another of its companies, Leamington & Warwick Electrical Co Ltd, where it was renumbered No 14.

Cheltenham car No 23 is seen at St Mark's depot, Cheltenham.
Courtesy A. D. Packer collection

Left: Leamington & Warwick No 14 is seen in Warwick.
Southerden, courtesy Roy Brook collection

Right: During March 1920, another Balfour Beatty company, Dumbarton Burgh & County Tramways Co Ltd, ordered two 72-seat double-deck tramcars, top-covered with open platforms. The cars were mounted on 8ft 0in Peckham P22 trucks with BTH electrical equipment, which comprised two GE 200K motors. The two cars, delivered in 1921, were given Fleet Nos 31 and 32.

Following closure of the Dumbarton system in 1928, the pair were sold to Ayr Corporation, which renumbered them 29 and 30. The cars were then sold to South Shields after the Ayr system was abandoned in 1932.

One of these cars, Ayr No 30, is seen waiting to return to Burns Monument.
Courtesy A. W. Brotchie collection

Below: Burnley Corporation in early 1920 ordered five new vestibuled single-deck tramcar bodies suitable for carrying 44 seated passengers. The cars, delivered in 1921, were numbered 68-72 and were mounted on Burnley bogies. In 1926 car No 68 was renumbered 73 to allow car No 10 to be renumbered 68 after being involved in an accident. 2 ACCIDENTS (1919 + 1923 AT SAME SPOT)

This busy scene in Burnley town centre shows car No 72 loading for Brunshaw, while the car on the right loading for Padiham is the new No 68.
Roy Brook collection

Above: Balfour Beatty & Co also placed orders in March 1920 for four bogie toastrack cars fitted with 4ft 1in wheelbase Preston equal wheel bogies for the Llandudno & Colwyn Bay Electric Railway, a 3ft 6in gauge line in North Wales. Again, BTH electrical gear was specified comprising two GE 249A motors and B 18 DD controllers.

The lift-over bench seats seated 60, and the front fixed lifeguards resembled cowcatchers on American railway locomotives. The cars, numbered 19-22, were completed in late 1920. They were 39ft long over platforms and the width over steps was 6ft 5in.

Car No 30 is seen in this official view taken at the Rhos depot. *EE*

Below: One of the cars is seen approaching the top of Penrhyn Hill from Llandudno with a full complement of passengers. *Sutton & Co (Rhos on Sea)/Author's collection*

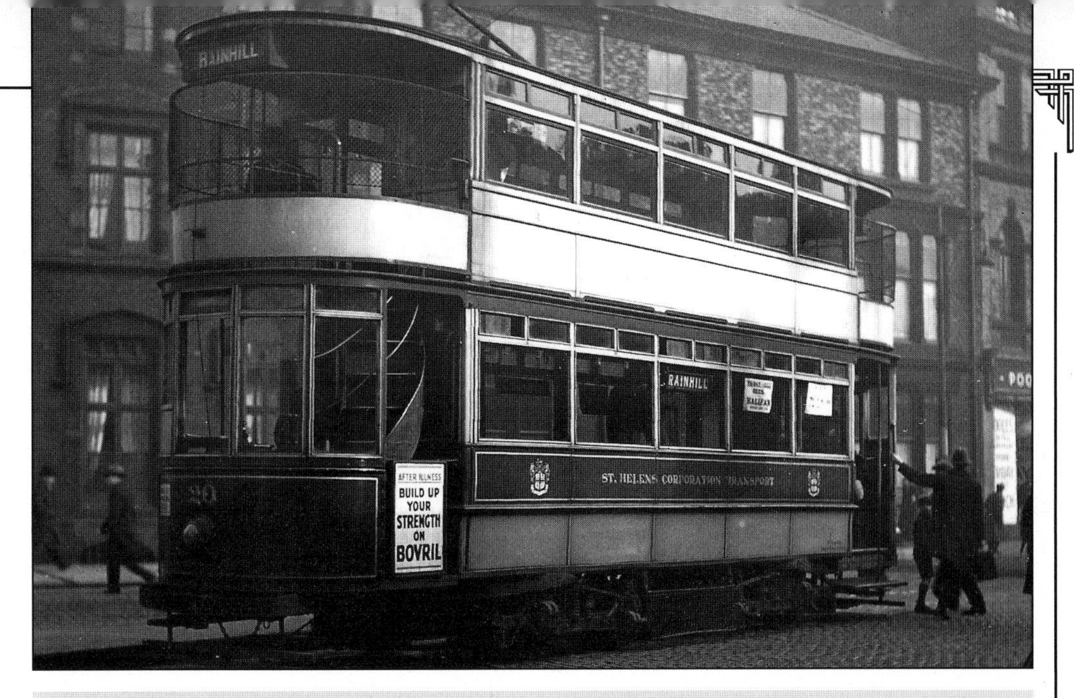

Above: St Helens Corporation on 1 October 1919 took over the operation of the St Helens & District Tramways Co Ltd. Included in the 36 trams acquired were four double-deck open-top bogie cars supplied by Dick, Kerr in 1918. In March 1920, St Helens ordered four new top covers from English Electric for these cars. EE records suggest that these were fitted to cars Nos 18-21. Car No 20, one of those top-covered in 1920, is seen loading for Rainhill, which was in July 1927 the first tram route to be converted to trolleybus operation. *NTM*

Below: In April 1920, Balfour Beatty & Co placed an order for two new tramcars for its subsidiary company, Llanelly & District Electric Supply Co Ltd. This time, they were conventional open-top cars seating 64 — 24 in the lower saloon. The cars were mounted on 8ft 0in wheelbase Peckham Pendulum P22 trucks with BTH electrical equipment comprising two GE 200K 40hp motors. These cars, delivered in late 1920, were numbered 15 and 16 and resembled the previous 14 cars.

Cars Nos 15 and 16 are seen inside the company's depot alongside one of the 1911 UEC-built cars (No 8). *Dr Hugh Nicol*

Above: Wolverhampton Corporation placed a repeat order in August 1920 for three further double-deck top-covered car bodies with open balconies. These were similar to the ones already supplied, but they were fitted for trolley pole collection instead of shoes for 'Lorain' stud collection.

Numbered 59-61, they were delivered to Wolverhampton in early 1921, two of the bodies being completed there to suit existing trucks that Wolverhampton was reusing. No 61 was photographed on test in Lea Road on the Penn Fields route during trials in 1921.
Bennett Clarke, courtesy D. Harvey collection

Left: South Lancashire Tramways Co continued its policy, started in 1916, of improving its tramcar fleet by purchasing in October 1920 a further three skeleton body frames complete with top decks for rebuilding existing four-wheel cars. At the same time, a further six canopy top covers were supplied by Preston for other four-wheel cars being modernised by the SLT Co where the existing bodies were being used. Examples of these rebuilt cars are shown in the two photographs.

Car 60 was photographed in July 1929 in Partington Lane near Swinton depot.
Dr H. Nicol, courtesy Roy Brook collection

Below right: Car 62 is *en route* to Atherton when seen in Ashton-in-Makerfield in 1928.
Dr H. A. Whitcombe, courtesy Roy Brook collection

Right: Northampton Corporation was the last customer to order new tramcars from English Electric in 1920, surprisingly specifying single-deck bogie cars with front exits instead of the traditional four-wheel double-deck cars bought previously. The four cars, Nos 34-7, seated 42 passengers and were mounted on Preston 22E maximum traction bogies. The electrical equipment comprised two 40hp DK30B motors and EE DB1-K3B controllers. Delivered in 1921, they were the last to be purchased. Car No 36 is shown.
W. J. S. Meredith, courtesy D. Harvey collection

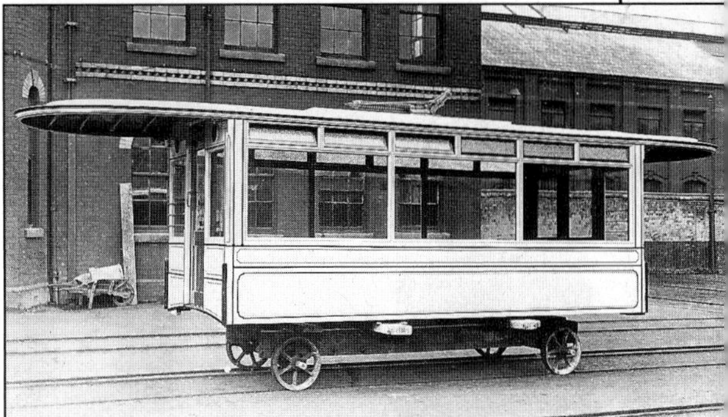

Centre right: The only tramcar order received during 1921 was for the supply of two more canopy top covers to the Dewsbury, Ossett & Soothill Nether Tramways, one of the subsidiaries of The National Electric Construction Co. The open balcony top covers were for fitting to cars built in 1908 by Brush. UEC had supplied two in 1915, and English Electric supplied two in both 1921 and 1925.

All eight were constructed to the same design, and the only differences were the running of the trolley cable under the roof on the last three covers. *EE*

Above: In 1912 Balfour Beatty replaced the 15 trams in the City of Carlisle Tramways Co Ltd fleet with 12 new cars from UEC. In both 1923 and 1925 English Electric supplied one new open tramcar top body to the same design as the 1912 cars. These bodies were fitted with existing trucks and numbered 15 and 14 respectively. One of these cars is seen in the closing years of the system, which was replaced by motorbuses in 1932 operated by the Ribble Motor Services.
Dr Hugh Nicol

Centre left: Car No 13 with a full load of passengers on the front at Morecambe.
unknown photographer /NTM collection

Below left: This view of car No 13 (where the number has been scribed on the glass plate at some time) is loading at Central Pier, Morecambe, before setting of for West End, while the competing Heysham & District Karrier open top double-deck motorbus overtakes on the nearside.
Alan A. Jackson/GLC

No photographs of Notts & Derby car Nos 1-3 fitted with new top covers in 1922 have bot been found.This is the only order not to be illustrated.

3 Reorganisation

When English Electric was formed in 1919, the various works were placed under central control based at the London office of Dick, Kerr & Co Ltd. During the first year, a new interim series of order numbers for work carried out at Preston was introduced whereby the number was prefixed by ET (Electric Traction) or C (Car Works). This series started at 10,000 and superseded the previous Car Works numbers which had ended with C1748 in early January 1919. (See EE build list 1.) When English Electric took over the London office, a second series of order numbers commencing at 50,000 was introduced. These were prefixed SC and had the suffix TWS (TramWay Section). This series was used from January 1920 until early 1922. (See EE build list 2.) During 1922 the Tramway Section moved to Preston and a third series of order numbers commencing at 5,000 was introduced, with prefix TY for home orders or TYX for export orders. All had the TWS suffix as before. This system continued until the reorganisation in 1933, when the Tramways Section was moved to Bradford.

At this time, the former United Electric Car Works on the east side of Strand Road was still involved with the production of bodies for all forms of transport, whilst the West Works still manufactured electrical equipment, ranging from tramcar equipment to massive turbines and generators of 20,000kW capacity for the new power stations then being built. Manufacture of equipment for electric locomotives of all sizes was undertaken at Preston, whilst the construction of chassis and bodywork was subcontracted to companies such as the North British Locomotive Co in Glasgow.

In 1920 the use of the tramcar for moving passengers had reached its peak. From then on, the use of tramways steadily declined due to the introduction of petrol-engined motorbuses, which were now becoming a reliable form of transport. The motorbus was also able to give the passengers a more comfortable ride, especially in comparison with the 1910 open-top type tramcars still used by many of the non-progressive tramway managers. Whilst 450 bodies had been

Below: Liverpool Overhead Railway had purchased three canopy top covers for existing tramcars in 1918 and placed a repeat order for a further one during August 1922. *EE*

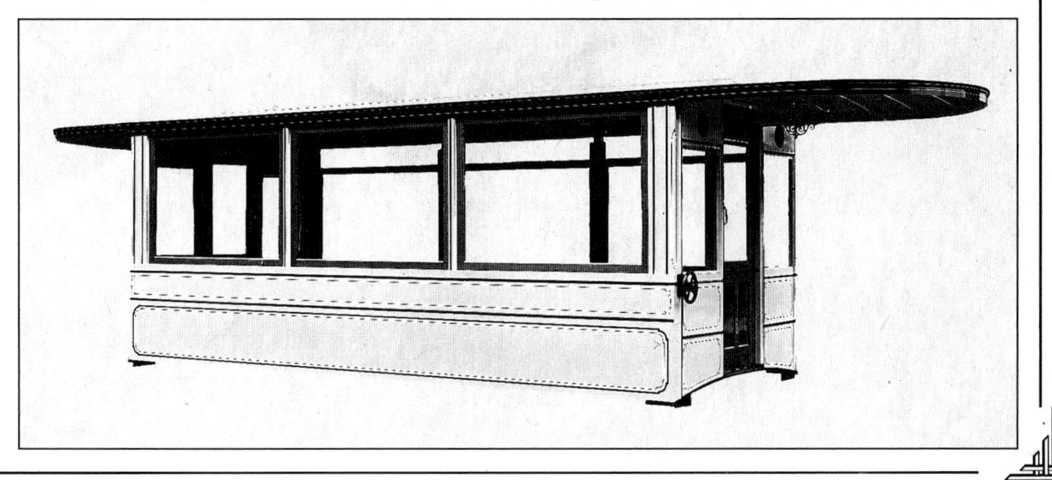

ordered during 1919 and 1920, the number ordered in 1921 and 1922 was 10, including the last two double-deck horse trams built by the company. These figures are for the British user, but export orders were also affected and in order to try to fill the void, the company accepted orders to build 40 motorbus bodies during those two years.

Between the beginning of 1923 and the end of 1930, orders for 622 car bodies were received from British customers, an average of 78 per year compared with 225 per year when the company was first formed. During the same period, a further 63 top covers were supplied to users wanting to improve their fleet to try to retain passengers.

Left: In October 1922, West Hartlepool Corporation ordered two double-deck open-top tramcar bodies for its 3ft 6in gauge system. The cars had vestibuled platforms and had accommodation for 64 passengers, 28 in the lower saloon.

Existing 22E trucks from earlier cars were reused by the Corporation, and the two cars, numbered 8 and 9, entered service in 1921. *EE*

Below left: In March 1923, Bolton Corporation placed an order for 10 double-deck unvestibuled bodies, with framing in English ash. Whilst the wheels and axles were supplied, the truck frames for the maximum traction bogies were provided by Bolton Corporation. The 82-seat cars seated 34 on the longitudinal seats in the lower saloon. The electrical equipment supplied comprised two 40hp DK20A2 motors and EE DB1-K3B controllers. Car No 126 was one of the 10 which were numbered 121-30. *Courtesy R. Marshall collection*

Left: Hull Corporation was one of the operators to consider unconventional new ideas. In March 1923 it placed an order for a totally enclosed tramcar mounted on a special Rayner 7ft 0in wheelbase truck built by English Electric, where the two 42hp DK85A motors were connected to gearboxes in the axles by long steel driving shafts.

The car body seated 64, with 24 on longitudinal seats in the lower saloon. One of the unusual features of the Hull system was the use of centre-grooved rails.

Car No 101 was delivered in 1923 and the photograph shows the shaft drive. *EE*

Below: Car No 101 in service. *Watson Bros/Author's collection*

Above: In 1923-4 South Lancashire Tramway Co ordered a total of seven new skeleton bodies for bogie cars complete with top covers, but unlike previous similar orders in 1916-8, it was specified that all pillars and middle rails must be made of teak rather than ash.

SLT completed the unvestibuled cars at its Atherton works, and the cars carried the fleet numbers of the ones providing trucks and electrical equipment, although four of the seven had new EMB Burnley bogies. This meant that although a car was listed in the company records as a 1906 Milnes bogie car, it was in fact a new car with refurbished running gear.

When the system closed, however, the bodies were advertised in 1933 as '12 Bogie Cars with teak bodies, drop windows on the top deck, WT 32 type GEC Motors, box type with roller bearings (purchased 1927). All in excellent condition.' This advert included the two completely new 1927 cars, Nos 44 and 45; therefore the other 10 must have been from the batch of 13 cars numbered 46-58. Cars Nos 51 and 52 were known not to have been top covered.

The identity of the eight cars sold to Bolton, which included the two new cars Nos 44 and 45 and six of the seven 1923-4 rebuilds numbered 47, 48, 50, 54, 55 and 58.

SLT car No 54 is seen at Ashton-in-Makerfield in 1929. *Dr Hugh Nicol*

Left: SLT car No 58. *Roy Brook collection*

Right and centre right: In May 1923, the contracting division of English Electric, the Consolidated Construction Co Ltd, placed an order with Preston for 25 new single-deck tramcars for the Dearne District Light Railways system, which they were building for the Wombwell, Wath upon Dearne, Bolton upon Dearne and Thurnscoe Urban District Councils. The system, centred on Wath upon Dearne, served routes extending over 18 route miles.

The 32ft-long cars, 6ft 6in wide, seated 36 passengers on the longitudinal bench seats and were mounted on Preston Peckham Pendulum four-wheel trucks with a wheelbase of 8ft 6in. The electrical equipment comprised two 40hp DK30B motors and type DB1-K3B controllers.

Delivery commenced in April 1924, and the system was officially opened on 10 July 1924, regular services beginning on 14 July 1924. This was the last new tramway system to be introduced in Britain until the introduction of Metrolink in Manchester in 1992. A further five cars were ordered in June 1924, and these were delivered in 1925.

Cars 1 and 17 are seen at Preston. *EE*

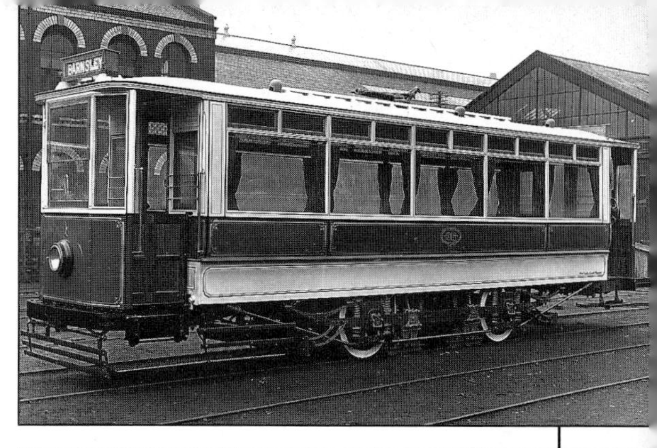

Below: Car No 30 is seen in Montgomery Road, Wath-upon-Dearne, with one of the competing Barnsley & District motorbuses.
Roy Brook collection

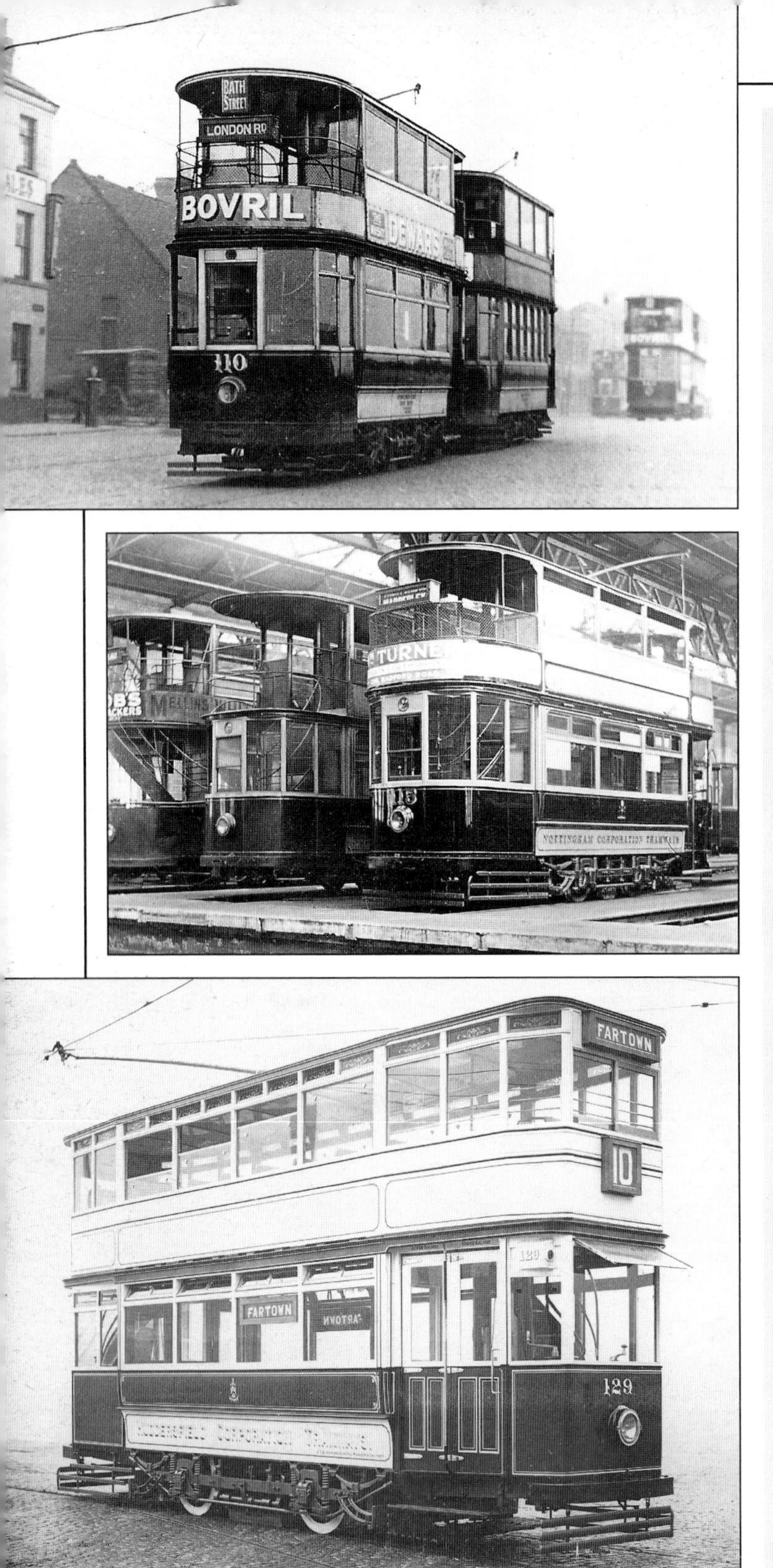

Left: Nottingham Corporation's Trent Bridge Works were kept busy for many years rebuilding a large proportion of its original fleet of trams. Between 1919 and 1924, English Electric supplied 55 lower saloon bodies, 22 of which had lower saloon platforms and vestibules. The other cars were fitted with platform vestibules by Henry Street & Co Ltd, coachbuilders at Muckham Street, Nottingham.

Typical of these rebuilds is car No 110, one of the cars with new EE lower saloon and Street vestibules.
G. H. F. Atkins

Centre left: Car No 115 was fitted with one of the 22 new English Electric lower deck body assemblies supplied in 1923 and 1924 with vestibules and canopy seats. Alongside No 115 is an unnumbered, partially converted car, together with No 18 awaiting its new lower deck. *G. H. F. Atkins*

Below left: When Huddersfield Corporation extended its tramway system in March 1923 to Brighouse, it found that its fleet of 126 tramcars was insufficient at times to meet peak demands, so in July 1923 a further 10 cars were ordered. This time, totally enclosed cars were specified, being an updated version of the 1920 cars, with trucks and electrical equipment being identical. However, they were the first cars to be delivered with roller blind route number boxes. The cars numbered 127-36 were delivered in late 1923. Car No 129 is depicted when new, fitted with C. H. Spencer slipper brakes. *EE*

Above: Plymouth Corporation, having acquired the Devonport & District Tramways Co in October 1915, and the Plymouth, Stonehouse & Devonport Tramway Co in July 1922, found it necessary to improve its rolling stock; therefore in October 1923 it ordered 20 new double-deck tramcar bodies with open tops and vestibuled platforms. Plymouth provided the 3ft 6in gauge 7ft 0in wheelbase type 21E trucks, whilst the two type 265 motors on each car were provided by BTH. The cars, numbered 131-50, were delivered in early 1924.

Car No 137 is seen in the unusual yellow and cream livery used by the Corporation between 1922 and 1927 outside the Milehouse depot with examples of the Corporation's first motorbuses parked behind. *EE*

Below: Car No 146 is seen on route 3, which linked Devonport (Morice Square) with the city centre by a circuitous route.
Southerden, courtesy Roy Brook collection

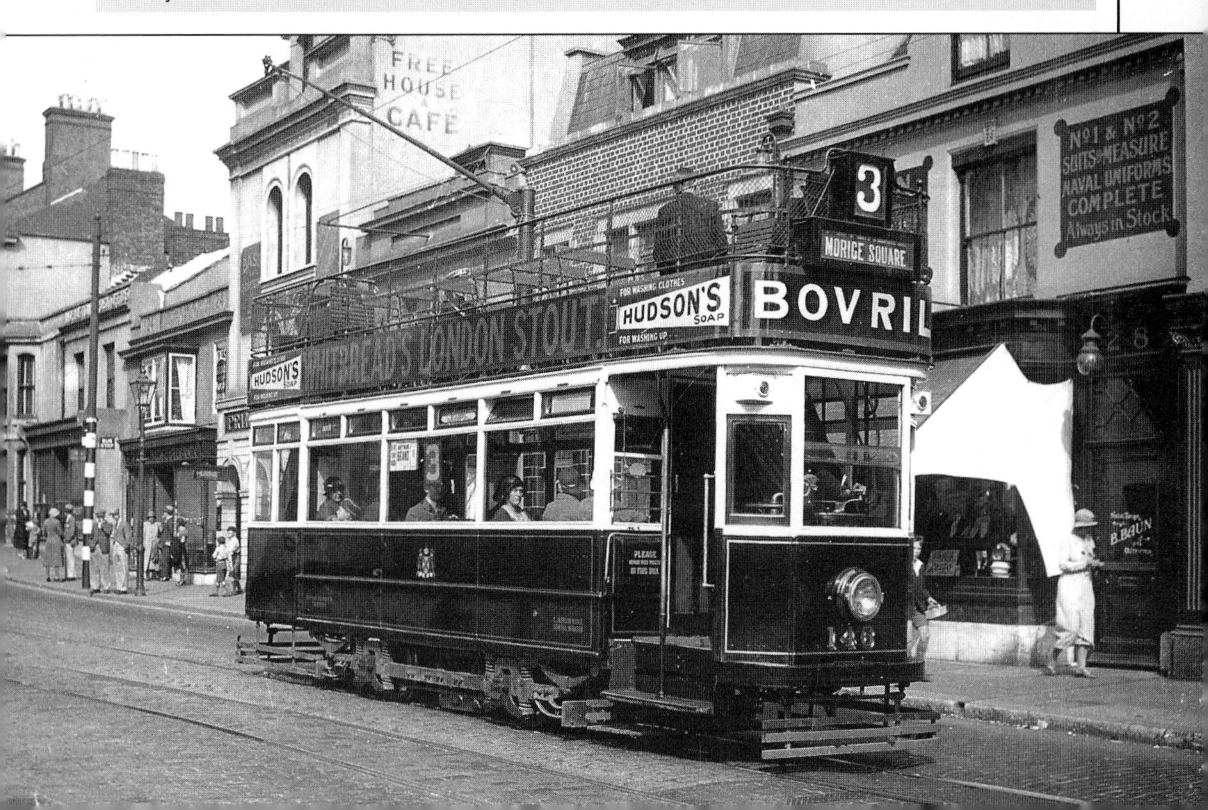

left: In August 1923, Lytham St Annes Borough Tramways ordered 10 new top-covered unvestibuled double-deck tramcars. The 31ft 0in-long cars were 7ft 0in wide and seated 61 passengers. The 23 seats in the lower saloon included 15 reversible back seats arranged with double and single seats on either side of the gangway. Whilst all the seats in the lower saloon were leather covered, those upstairs were of the traditional wood-slatted reversible type. Even though the cars were known as Pullman cars, their appearance was far from modern.

The trucks were 8ft 6in wheelbase Peckham Pendulum type P22 which cost £175 each and were purchased direct by the undertaking. The electrical equipment was purchased from Preston and comprised two DK84B 32hp motors and EE DB1-K3 controllers. The electrical equipment cost £488 per car, and the bodies £1,050 each. The cars were delivered in February and March 1924, and became Fleet Nos 41-50.

Car 43 is seen leaving Talbot Square, Blackpool, when new. *Courtesy Roy Brook collection*

Centre left: Car No 44 is seen in Clifton Square, Lytham, sporting the modern style livery introduced in 1932 with Lytham St Annes Corporation fleetname. *R. Elliott*

Below left: In August 1923, Salford Corporation purchased 10 canopy-type top covers for fitting to existing tramcars originally built in 1913-4 by Brush.

Car No 159 is seen with EE top cover working on route 33 from Swinton church to Deansgate. *M. J. O'Connor, courtesy A. D. Packer*

Right: Oldham Corporation was the first customer to order new cars in 1924, this time specifying six totally enclosed double-deck cars seating 64 passengers, with the usual longitudinal seats for 22 in the lower saloon and 42 narrow-slat garden types in the upper saloon.

Again, they were mounted on Preston 7ft 6in wheelbase type 21E trucks with CH Spencer 'Huddersfield' type slipper brakes. The electrical equipment comprised two DK30B 40hp motors and EE K33B controllers. The cars, numbered 17-20, 22 and 24, entered service between late June and July 1924. *EE*

Below: The County Borough of Southend-on-Sea ordered six double-deck bogie tramcars with enclosed tops in January 1924. The cars seated 70, with 34 downstairs on longitudinal seats, and were mounted on EE Burnley maximum traction bogies. Electrical equipment comprised two DK30B 40hp motors and EE DB1-K3B controllers.

Car No 57 is seen when new in Southend in September 1924. *EE*

Left: Edinburgh Corporation's January 1924 order was for the supply of 20 top-covered double-deck bodies with lower saloon vestibules for Edinburgh to complete using Metro-Vickers and BTH equipment. This batch became Fleet Nos 312-31.

This photograph of car No 323 with background deleted was used in EE publicity. *EE*

Below: Car No 325 is seen in June 1949 at the art gallery and shows the extent of the rebuilding carried out in the 1930s to give them a more modern image. *M. H. Waller/ A. W. Brotchie collection*

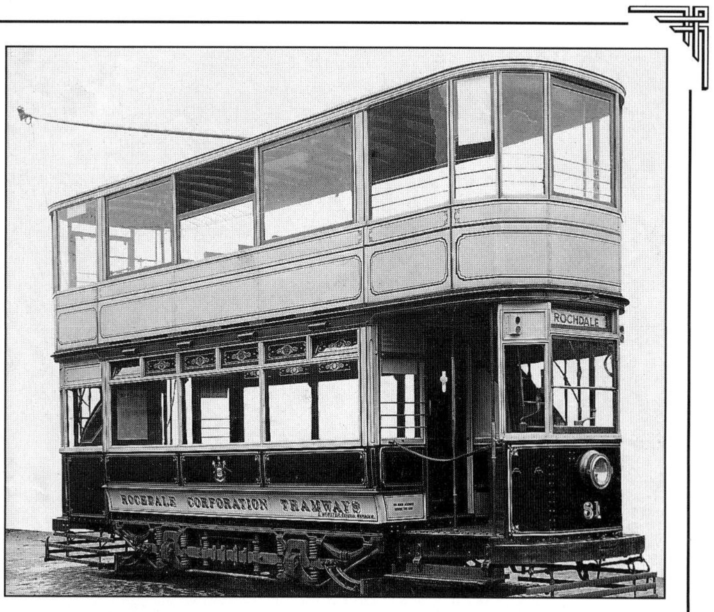

Right: In August 1924, Rochdale Corporation placed its first order for totally enclosed tramcars. These were an updated version of the 1920-built cars, having the same type of trucks and equipment. The cars seated 64.

The elimination of the upper saloon bulkhead partition allowed the upstairs seating arrangement to be modified to accommodate 42, instead of 36. Car No 81 is seen in Rochdale following reassembly and testing. *EE*

Above: Southend-on-Sea Corporation Tramways, obviously pleased with its new cars delivered in 1924, placed a further order in September 1924 for six enclosed canopy top-covers for existing bogie cars Nos 18-22 built in 1904 by Milnes, and for car No 23 built in 1909 by UEC.

A second order was placed a month later, this time for a further five enclosed canopy-top covers for two more 1909 UEC cars, Nos 24 and 25, and three for the 1912 Brush cars, Nos 37-9, again, all bogie cars.

All these 11 cars received new EE DK30B 40hp motors, and EE K3B controllers, cars Nos 18-25 in 1924-5 and cars Nos 37-9 in 1927. Car 22 is shown fitted with its new top cover. *A. D. Packer*

Left: Pioneer solution tried at York: by 1924, many tramway operators had found that expenditure on operating costs and interest, and sinking fund charges, was greater than the revenue received from passengers. When Mr J. A. Bromley, the General Manager at York Corporation, was faced with this problem, it was losing some £2,000 per year operating a three-mile route. He concluded in a report that if the driver of the tram could collect fares as well as drive, the platform costs would drop by 50%, and a net profit of some £20 per annum could be made. The Ministry of Transport agreed to a six-month trial of an experimental one-man-operated tram, subject to it being limited to a seating capacity of 24.

York Corporation placed an order with EE for the supply of a front entrance 'one-man' single-deck tram mounted on a 6ft 0in wheelbase Preston standard four-wheel truck suitable for the 3ft 6in gauge system. The electrical equipment comprised two 30hp DK29A motors and DB1-K3 controllers.

The car was 23ft 6in long and the total weight was 8 tons 7cwt.The underframe was fabricated from steel sections whilst the body was constructed using ash for pillars and framework. Trolley reversers had been installed on the system so that operation was as simple as possible. The passengers entered and left using the front entrance. An interior partition in the body segregated passengers smoking — they had to use the rear saloon. The driver sat on a circular seat which enabled him to have full control of the car. Westinghouse air brakes were fitted and these were also arranged to operate in conjunction with the dead man control gear on the controller.

The car — No 37 — entered service in late 1925, and by 1928 had been converted into a works car. *Courtesy Roy Brook collection*

Centre left: In March 1925, West Ham Corporation placed an order with EE for six double-deck bogie tramcar bodies with enclosed balconies and open platforms. Seating was provided for 78 passengers. The cars, numbered 119-25, were placed into service in the autumn of 1925. West Ham was taken over in 1933, when the London Passenger Transport Board was formed, and the cars were renumbered 325-30 by the LPTB.

Car No 119 is seen at Stratford pre-1933. *Courtesy F. P. Groves collection*

Below left: Car No 121, renumbered 327 by the LPTB, is seen in July 1938 in West Ham. *H. B. Priestley, courtesy F. P. Groves*

Right: At the beginning of 1925, Manchester Corporation placed an order with EE for 60 more cars. These became Fleet Nos 934-93 and were placed into service progressively between July 1925 and October 1926. The cars were mounted on EMB-supplied Manchester type bogies.

Car No 962 is seen at Manchester Exchange station on 11 August 1948.
M. H. Waller, courtesy A. D. Packer

Below: In May 1925, Bury Corporation placed orders with Preston for six new totally enclosed tramcars, and six vestibuled top covers for 1903 Milnes cars, which the Corporation was rebuilding using kits of parts supplied by Preston. These kits included 'vestibule ends, staircases, tool lockers and all furniture required to equip customer's existing open cars with covers and vestibules similar to the six new cars'. In March 1926, a further eight sets of conversion material were ordered, this time including drivers' platforms, railings and canopies as well as eight pairs of Burnley bogie trucks complete with axles, but without wheels and tyres, which Bury supplied. All these 20 cars seated 80, with 32 being accommodated on the traditional longitudinal closed slat type side bench seat in the lower saloon. The new cars were numbered 55-60, whilst the 14 'lookalikes' retained numbers 1-14.

How much of the original Milnes body survived is anybody's guess, but similar bodies at South Lancashire Tramways had by then already been replaced by new body shells.

The electrical equipment used on all 20 comprised two 46hp GEC WT32H motors and EE K3B controllers.

Car No 58 is seen in Bury in the winter of 1925.
EE

Right: Car No 13 is at Walmersley terminus on 9 October 1948. *M. H. Waller, courtesy A. D. Packer*

Left: In 1925, Balfour Beatty & Co ordered two new double-deck enclosed canopy open-platform tramcar bodies for its subsidiary company, Mansfield & District Light Railway Co.

The order specified teak construction, and when built, they were arranged to seat 74 passengers: the lower saloon longitudinal seats accommodated 28, whilst seating for 46 was provided upstairs on garden narrow-slat reversible seats. However, it must be noted that later sources suggest that the seating was reduced to 26/40.

The Peckham P22 trucks and BTH electrical equipment were not included in the order.

After the closure of the system at Mansfield in October 1932, cars Nos 27 and 28 were sold to Sunderland Corporation, becoming their Nos 21 and 24. Car No 27 is seen outside Mansfield depot when new. *EE*

Right: Car No 27 is seen in the early 1950s as Sunderland 21, Sunderland having carried out various alterations including fitting new EMB hornless trucks and equipment. By then, the lower saloon seated 24 on upholstered seats, whilst the upper saloon still had 40 wooden seats. *Roy Brook*

Right: In October 1925, after taking delivery of its first totally enclosed cars, Rochdale placed orders for a further four complete cars and three new bodies for fitting on to existing trucks and electrical equipment salvaged from withdrawn cars. The first four became Fleet Nos 86-9, whilst the hybrids became Nos 90-2.

One of the trucks for Nos 86-9 is seen outside the car works. *EE*

Below: Car No 87 is seen outside Rochdale's Mellor Street depot in 1926. *EE*

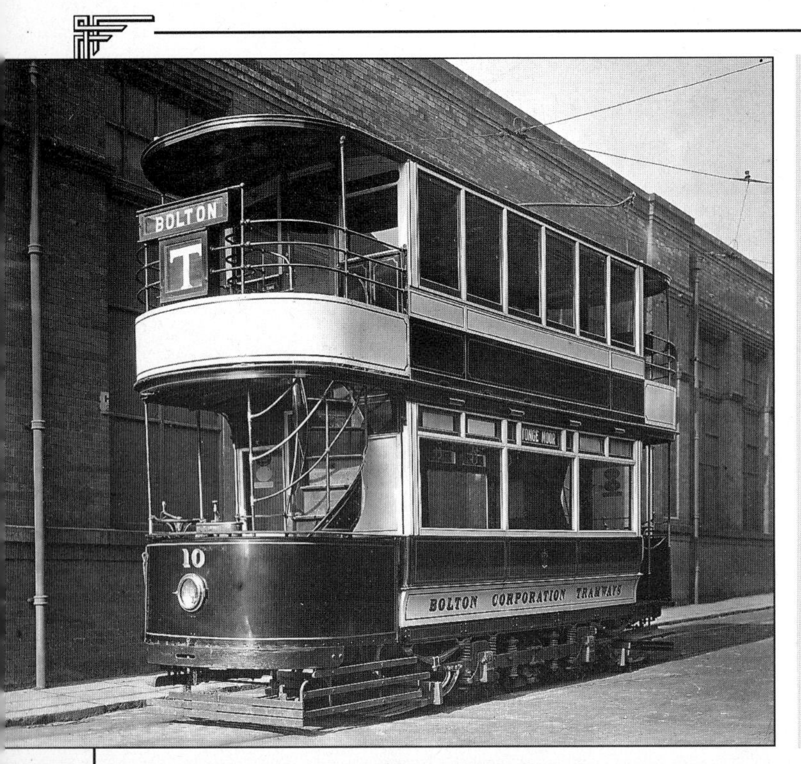

Left: Bolton Corporation had purchased its first 40 open-top tramcars from ER&TCW at Preston in 1899, all of which were fitted with balcony top covers by 1914. In 1924, EE supplied four new top covers as replacements. The following year, Bolton ordered three new top-covered unvestibuled 58-seat car bodies to replace the bodies on cars Nos 8, 9 and 10. These seated 22 in the lower saloon and 28 in the upper saloon, with the remaining eight being accommodated, four on each balcony, on wooden slat seats.

Car No 10 is seen outside Bolton's Bradshawgate depot in 1926 after assembly using existing trucks and equipment. *EE*

Below: Also taken at the same time, this view shows the lower saloon interior on Car No 10. *EE*

Right: Oldham Corporation was another customer to order new tramcars in late 1925. Like the Bolton order, it was for three window cars seating 62 passengers, made possible by having vestibules without upper saloon bulkhead partitions. The cars were mounted on Preston 21E standard trucks with Oldham wide-wing axle boxes and C. H. Spencer 'Huddersfield' type slipper brakes. Electrical equipment comprised two 40hp DK30B motors and DB1-K33B controllers.

These 12 cars were delivered in 1926 to Oldham and carried Fleet Nos 121-32.

This works photograph, taken in February 1926, shows the lower saloon body framework for one of Oldham's 12 cars. *EE*

Below: Two of the cars, the front one No 122, are seen outside Oldham's depot on a very wintry day. *A. D. Packer*

Above: The largest single order which EE received for tramcar bodies was obtained in November 1925, when Leeds City Tramways placed an order for 75 totally enclosed double-deck car bodies costing £1,390 each. At the same time, Brush received a similar order for 75 car bodies, their price being £1,397 each. The EE cars, Leeds Nos 76-150, were placed into service between July 1926 and June 1927.

The cars were 31ft 2in long, 7ft 1in wide and seated 26 downstairs on leather-upholstered longitudinal seats. Forty-six were accommodated upstairs, 32 on reversible seats and the others on fixed canopy seats at each end of the upper saloon. The teak-framed bodies were finished internally to a high standard, and Leeds City Tramways leased premises belonging to Kitson's at Hunslet to reassemble the 150 cars.

Car No 87 is seen in St Chad's Road, Headingley, in the later blue livery. *Roy Brook*

Left: Car No 77 is seen in October 1952 after being repainted into the later crimson livery. *R. Wiseman, courtesy Roy Brook collection*

Right: In April 1926, Nottingham Corporation ordered 20 totally enclosed double-deck car bodies, suitable for seating 70 passengers. The lower saloon, like the Leeds cars, had 24 seats upholstered in leather, each side having four cushions, whilst the upper saloon again had seating for 46. The trucks were not supplied but the electrical equipment, comprising two 40hp DK30B motors and EE DB1-K33B controllers, was.

This was the last tramcar order placed by Nottingham, having already ordered its first 10 trolleybuses from Railless Ltd, which purchased its electrical equipment from English Electric. The cars, numbered 181-200, were delivered during late 1926 and early 1927. Eighteen of these cars, numbered 181-94 and 196-9, were sold to Aberdeen Corporation in 1936 following the closure of the Nottingham system.

Car No 183 was photographed in Nottingham for EE. *EE*

Above: The changeover from tram to motorbus or trolleybus was recorded by G. H. F. Atkins, whose superb photographs captured the atmosphere of the period. Car No 181 is seen in traffic heading for the city from Trent Bridge, along with a dual-door AEC Reliance bus and trolleybus. This tram route was closed in May 1934. *G. H. F. Atkins*

Right: In May 1926, Manchester Corporation placed another order with EE, this time for 50 more totally enclosed double-deck tramcars to a similar specification to previous orders built at Preston. They were allocated Fleet Nos 1004-53, and the first one to enter service in April 1927 was 1007, which also became the last tram to operate in Manchester when the system closed on 10 January 1949. It took 12 months before the last of the 50 entered service. This view of the upper saloon interior shows the improved type of seating introduced by then, and the front window proudly displays a picture proclaiming 'Manchester Goods — Manchester Docks'. *EE*

Below: No 1007 is seen on 11 August 1948 at Exchange station with the conductor turning the trolley on service 37x to Levenshulme. *M H Waller, courtesy A. D. Packer*

Above: When, on Monday 10 January 1949, Manchester waved farewell to the tram, nobody expected that 43 years later, a new car No 1007 would open a new tramway system in Manchester.

This view shows the civic party in 1949 talking to driver Bob Berwick prior to departure at 11.30am of car No 1007 for the depot in Birchfields Road. *Author's collection*

Right: In July 1926, Rochdale Corporation ordered a fully enclosed top cover from English Electric suitable for mounting onto an existing body which Rochdale was rebuilding as a 64-seat car with 42 of the seats on the top deck. This 'new' Rochdale-built car entered service numbered 93. A further identical car numbered 94 followed in 1928 (illustrated overleaf).

Car No 93 is seen at Rochdale Town centre in 1927. *F. P. Groves*

Left: Car No 94 is seen in Rochdale town centre in 1932. *F. P. Groves*

Below: Bolton Corporation ordered 12 totally enclosed double-deck tramcar bodies complete with electric control equipment suitable for mounting on Brill maximum traction 22E bogies to be supplied by Brush. Seating was provided for 77 passengers, 29 in the lower saloon accommodated on four double corner seats facing the central gangway and seven rows of double and single reversible cross seats. The cars, numbered 139-50, were delivered in 1927. Car No 144 is shown in an official publicity photograph. *EE*

Right: The lower saloon interior of car No 144 shows the improved seating layout. *EE*

Below right: Car No 145 is seen in Bolton town centre in December 1933. The AEC Q-type double-deck bus was the centre of attraction, whilst the other vehicles provide an interesting glimpse of the past. *Author's collection*

ALEXANDRE
ENGLANDS
TAILORS
FRANK CLO
MONTSERRAT
145
MARKLAND HILL
10
WH 4850

Above: South Lancashire Tramways Co placed an order for two top-covered double-deck bogie cars in January 1927. The cars, with open vestibules, were practically identical to the various SLT rebuilds introduced during the previous 10 years. The cars, numbered 44 and 45, were mounted on EMB Burnley bogies obtained direct by SLT. Motors were supplied by GEC, but EE supplied DB1-K33C controllers. These two cars were sold to Bolton Corporation in 1933.

This view of car No 44, seen when new, makes an interesting comparison with other recent bogie cars built by EE for more progressive users. *EE*

Left and right: These views of the interior of the two saloons on car No 44 make interesting comparisons with the views shown earlier of cars supplied to Bolton, Manchester and Oldham. *EE*

Above: The other order received in 1927 was from Norwich Electric Tramways Co, which ordered a further four double-deck open-top, open platform tramcar bodies complete with new EE DB1-K33B controllers. Trucks were provided by the client, who re-used the old motors. Between 1923 and 1930, Norwich placed nine orders for a total of 34 cars to be replaced this way.

Car No 15 was one of four cars rebodied in 1927, and is seen in January 1928 at the Silver Road depot, Norwich, ready to re-enter service still looking like the 1899-1900 car it replaced. *EE*

Blackpool Corporation 'Pullman' Cars — The 'Pantographs'

Above: In February 1928, Blackpool Corporation placed an order with English Electric for 10 new single-deck bogie tramcars costing £2,000 each. The cars, 40ft long, were 7ft 6in wide, and the saloons were built with a clear internal height of 7ft 6in.

The order specified that the cars were to have capacity for 50 seated passengers: 44 in the saloon and six on the platforms. A month later this was amended to four on the platforms. The cars were mounted on 4ft 1in wheelbase equal wheel bogies with 30in diameter wheels, and the electrical equipment specified was two GEC WT28L 50hp motors and BTH B510 pattern controllers.

The construction of the body was unusual: to avoid the problems with draughts from windows and conventional ventilators, a clerestory roof reminiscent of late 1890s railway carriages was incorporated into the roof structure of the body, which was teak framed on a steel underframe.

The roof structure was constructed using ash roof sticks, mountings and top and bottom rails, and boarded with tongue-and-groove pine boards. To keep the weather out and provide flexibility, the entire roof was covered with white lead paint, with the roofing canvas laid on top whilst the paint was still wet. Further coats of white lead paint provided a weather seal. The author is the owner of a 1928 English Electric motor bus body which is constructed with bodywork in the same style.

Delivery of the cars, numbered 167-76, began in July 1928, and they were all placed into service in October 1928. An unusual requirement of the order was the supply of emergency oil lamps to be carried on each platform.

Car No 167 is seen at Fleetwood Ferry on 3 August 1933, still running with only one tail lamp in the platform dash. By then, the car had been painted into the green and cream livery, which was lined out in gold on the green, and green and black on the cream. *R. Elliott*

Above: In 1959, cars Nos 169 and 175 were still in the green and cream livery introduced in 1945. However, when last repainted in 1957, the old shaded numerals were replaced by Gill Sans numerals. The cars are seen at Blackpool's South Pier and Bath Terminus when both cars were being used for enthusiasts special tours. *Author*

Left: Circa 1947, car No 175 is seen at Fleetwood Ferry working the Fleetwood local service to Broadwater. By then, it had two tail lights and a trolley pole, but was still painted in the 1937-style livery, which was mainly cream with a green roof and window surrounds. *Roy Brook*

Right: Blackpool car No 167 was taken out of service in July 1953 and converted into a permanent way car. This 1955 view shows it at Copse Road, Fleetwood, together with the Corporation's 1927 electric locomotive, also built by English Electric. *Roy Brook*

Above: In May 1924 English Electric carried out tests on the Blackpool-Fleetwood tramway system using two Blackpool Corporation tramcars fitted with prototype equipment suitable for multiple-unit operation of two powered cars under the control of one motorman.

The first customer to purchase this type of equipment was the British Columbia Electric Railway of Vancouver. One of the British managers, who was an enthusiastic supporter of Continental tramways which used multiple-units and trailers, was Mr P. Priestly, who in 1925-6 was President of the Municipal Tramways Association and Chairman of its Joint Committee on Tramways Rolling Stock. He had been the General Manager at Liverpool since 1920, and had recommended the use of Continental type trams. Liverpool Corporation was discussing schemes involving the use of single-deck tramcars in a possible subway in Everton and the planned tunnel under the Mersey. A prototype single-deck bogie tramcar suitable for use with a trailer or for multiple-unit operation was ordered from English Electric in 1928.

The car, 37ft 0in long and 7ft 2in wide, was very similar to the Pantograph cars then being built for Blackpool. The requirements for it, to operate over 35ft 0in radius curves, meant that the wheelbase was 17ft 6in, one foot shorter than the Blackpool cars. This necessitated altering the spacing of the body pillars to suit, hence the side windows were not all the same length. The car was mounted on two 4ft 2in wheelbase Monomotor bogies, where all the wheels were powered from the single 60hp DK120 motor on each bogie.

The car was delivered to Liverpool as fleet No 757 in July 1929 and was placed into service in October 1929. It was well liked by the travelling public and was capable of spirited performance. The big disadvantage was the narrow entranced doorway, short platforms and the narrow gangway, which meant time was wasted unloading and loading passengers at stops. This unique car was in use until 1935 when its non-standard features caused its withdrawal.

A Liverpool photographer caught Blackpool Corporation enclosed car No 121 and open car No 122 in May 1924 during the EE tests carried out from Bispham depot. *Stewart Bale*

Right: Liverpool car No 757 is seen when new in 1929. *MPTE, courtesy Roy Marshall collection*

122
SPECIAL
LIVERPOOL CORPORATION TRAMWAYS
757

Above: In July 1928, Coventry Corporation ordered five double-deck top-covered tramcars with open-ended balconies. These 52-seat cars were provided with 24 moquette-upholstered longitudinal seats in the lower saloon. In the upper saloon, 23 passengers were seated on leather-upholstered seats, and each balcony was fitted with wooden canopy seats for four. When delivered in 1929, the cars were numbered 64-8.

Car No 64 is seen soon after delivery to Coventry. *EE*

Left: The upper saloon of car No 64 shows the seating arrangements. *EE*

Above: Car No 68 is seen in service in the 1930s.
Courtesy D. Harvey collection

Right: In the summer of 1928, Bolton Corporation ordered a further three totally enclosed double-deck tramcar bodies, similar to the ones supplied in spring 1927. They are believed to have been delivered by the end of 1928 and were given the numbers of the recently withdrawn single deck tramcars 104-106. In 1940, Bolton renumbered its remaining tram fleet by adding 300 to the number.
No 406, former 106, is seen in Trinity Street, Bolton, in 1945.
Burrows Bros, courtesy
F. P. Groves collections

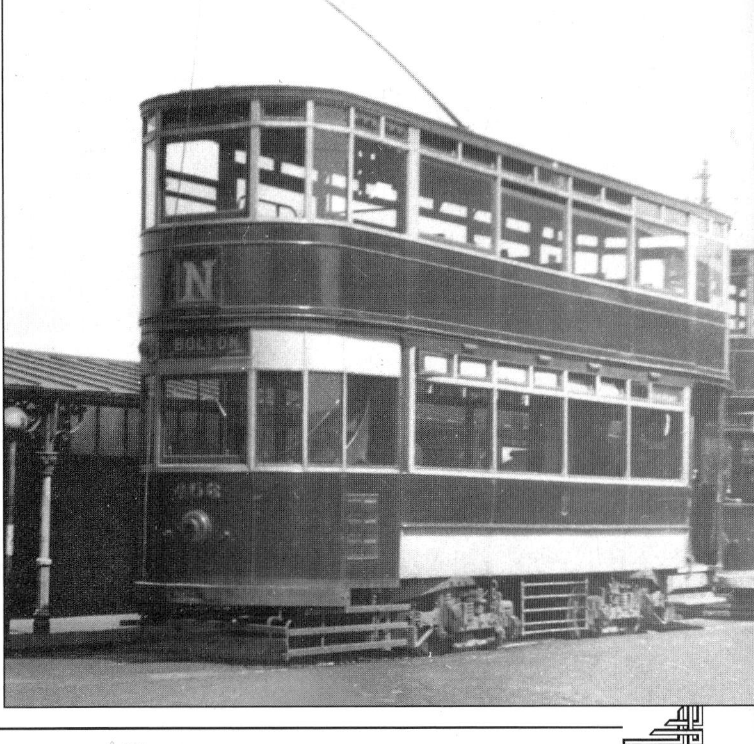

ALDWYCH AND ISLINGTON VIA KINGSWAY AND ROSEBERY AVENUE
L. C. C.

FULL
AUBREY LLEWELLYN COVENTRY FELL. TRAMWAYS MANAGER.

Previous page: The only large order received by EE in 1928 was from London County Council for 50 new double-deck tramcar bodies which were to be mounted on the 50 sets of maximum traction bogies and electrical equipment salvaged from the 16 class F and 34 class G single-deck bogie cars being withdrawn when the Kingsway Subway was closed for enlargement to take double-deck cars. The withdrawn cars, numbered 552-601, received new bodies and were then reclassified as class E/1. The thicker centre window pillar in the lower saloon indicated that they were not one of the original 1,000 class E/1 cars. Delivered without drivers' windscreens, they were fitted in the late 1930s. One of the 16 class F single-deck cars No 563 is seen when new in 1905. *Hoole UEC*

Left: While car No 600 is one of the 50 new cars using the salvaged equipment. *R. Elliott*

Right: London County Council placed the only major tramcar order to be received by EE in 1929, for the supply of 50 double-deck tramcar bodies for new bogie cars (class HR2). These were an updated version of the bodies supplied to them earlier that year. These cars were built with all-metal bodywork, and by having slab side panels it allowed a transverse seating layout to be included in the lower saloon.

The 74-seat cars had provision for 28 on transverse moquette seats in the lower saloon, and 46 on transverse leather cloth-covered seats in the upper saloon. The cars, numbered 1854-1903, entered service from August 1930.

One of the lower saloons is seen under construction at Preston, showing the all-metal bodyshell panelled with sheet steel. *EE*

Lower right: These cars were fitted with drivers' vestibules in the 1930s. This view of car No 1885 shows how the slab sides gave the cars a modern look. *V. C. Jones, courtesy IAL*

Left: 1929 was another poor year for the car works. Norwich Electric Tramways Co placed two orders during the year for a total of six open-top double-deck car bodies. Halifax Corporation placed two orders for new tramcars mounted on 7ft 6in wheelbase Peckham trucks with EE DK30/1L motors and EE DB1-K33E controllers. The first order for seven cars was received in January 1929, with a repeat order for a further three following in November 1929.

The bodies were built to the design of the Halifax Corporation manager, Mr W. T. Young. His prototype, car No 107, had been built in 1927 and after trials over the 3ft 6in gauge system, production of a further 20 followed from the Corporation's own workshops and from English Electric. The 29ft 4in-long cars were 6ft 6in wide, and because of the narrow gauge and problems in operating routes in high winds past exposed places, the overall height of these cars was 15ft 5in, some 15in lower than previous cars. These trams were believed to be the first in the country to be fitted with semi-bucket back, fully upholstered reversible tramcar seats, manufactured in the Halifax area by Siddall & Hilton Ltd. The teak-framed bodies were mounted on a steel underframe.

The first seven English Electric cars were numbered initially 6, 28, 95, 20, 33 and 15 (then to 114-20) and the last three, delivered in 1930, carried numbers 121-3. One of the English Electric cars numbered in the first number series above is seen here in Halifax before its renumbering. *EE*

Left: 1930 was another poor year for trams. Rochdale Corporation, in an attempt to keep passengers, purchased 11 new unvestibuled canopy top covers for existing cars. Five of these were for four-wheel cars, and the other six were for bogie cars, Nos 44-9, built in 1905 by Brush.

Car No 45 is seen on the Esplanade at Rochdale after being top-covered. By 12 November 1932, Rochdale had withdrawn its tramcars and replaced them by motorbuses. *W. T. Carter, courtesy Roy Brook collection*

Below: Car No 10, one of the five four-wheel cars fitted with a new top cover, is seen in Rochdale town centre in 1930. *Burrows/F. P. Groves collection*

Above: A fire in April 1930 destroyed 11 cars at the Laxey depot of the Manx Electric Railway. Amongst these were a number of bogie toastrack trailers. The Manx Electric Railway quickly ordered three open cross-bench trailer car bodies, with seating being provided for 44 passengers on transverse pine lath seats. The three bodies were quickly built and supplied for the summer seasonal traffic, and carried the numbers of the burnt-out trailers, Nos 40, 41 and 44. Like the Blackpool Pantographs, the cars were equipped with oil lamps and electric signal lights. Trailer car No 40 poses for the camera. *EE*

Right: The interior of car No 40, showing open sides, wooden seats, clerestory roof and, at the end, the emergency and wheel brakes. *EE*

Above: Liverpool Corporation placed 12 new totally enclosed double-deck tramcars into service between October 1931 and June 1932. Whilst these cars, numbered 758-69, were known as 'English Electrics', English Electric supplied only the Monomotor bogies, costing £1,700 per set, control gear at £365 and £80 per set for the air brake equipment. For these 'English Electric' tramcars, the bodies were built by the Edge Lane works of Liverpool Corporation.

Each of the inside framed bogies had the larger DK131 66hp motor instead of the DK120 used on the single-deck car No 757 supplied two years earlier, but this time they were fitted with G. D. Peters & Co air brakes. Further similar cars were planned, but with the death of the Tramways Manager in March 1933, and the various teething problems with the Monomotor bogies, they were eventually built using a competitor's truck. 'English Electric' car No 758 is seen when new in October 1931. *MPTE, courtesy R. Marshall collection*

Above right: A similar EE Monomotor bogie supplied to London United for trials under Feltham car No 396 is seen at Preston in 1930. *S. Bale (Liverpool)*

Right: At the end of 1930, London County Council placed another order for 50 totally enclosed double-deck cars for fleet replacements at Leyton. These cars, classified E/3, were 33ft 10in long, 7ft 1in wide and were similar to the HR/2 cars already supplied, but having two 57½hp DK126A motors instead of the four 30hp MV109 motors on the HR/2.

E/3 car No 187 is seen in service on route 35 in Highgate on 29 February 1952. *A. D. Packer*

35
... but Hovis and butter is better
29 Furniture 29
ASPRO
ASPRO

Above: 1931 was another poor year for tramcar orders from home customers. The only one in May was for six new cars for Huddersfield Corporation, costing £2,486 each. These cars were 29ft 0in long overall and 7ft 0in wide. The teak-framed bodies were built on a steel and oak underframe, which was mounted on a Maley & Taunton 8ft 0in wheelbase truck equipped with M & T airwheel, airtrack and magnetic brakes. The electrical equipment comprised two DK105/5H 50hp motors and DB1-K33E controllers. The cars seated 60 passengers, with 20 in the lower saloon. Deliveries commenced in August 1931 and all six, numbered 137-42, were in service by late September.

Nine months later, in June 1932, a further two cars were ordered, numbered 143-4. This time, the bodies were built 1ft longer to give better seating distribution, which, according to the specification issued internally by EE, was still 20 in the lower saloon and 40 in the upper saloon, although the original enquiry and the EE quotation specified 20 and 42 respectively. These eight cars were the most luxurious in Huddersfield, with concealed lighting and luxuriously upholstered spring seats. The cars, capable of speeds up to 40mph, spent most of their time at Huddersfield on the long crosstown route linking Bradley to Marsden, two routes which suffered from extensive bus competition. In April 1938, following the closure of the Marsden part of this route, the eight cars were sold for £225 each to Sunderland Corporation.

Huddersfield car No 137 is seen outside the Great Northern Street works in September 1931 after final assembly and testing. *EE*

Right: No 144, one of the two cars ordered in June 1932, is seen in late 1932 following delivery to Huddersfield. *Greaves/Author's collection*

Centre right: Sunderland car No 35, formerly Huddersfield No 139, is seen in service in 1953. Sunderland had removed the platform doors and fitted a pantograph before placing them in service. *Roy Brook*

Below right: During November 1932, Sunderland ordered nine double-deck totally enclosed tramcar bodies from Preston to designs based on car No 86, which had been built by the Corporation and placed into service during September.

These cars, numbered 87-95, entered service during the summer of 1933. They were mounted on EMB hornless roller-bearing trucks with a wheelbase of 8ft 6in, and seating for 62 passengers was provided on upholstered seats. Car No 88 is seen working the Durham Road route in 1953. *Roy Brook*

Progress at Blackpool — The Streamliners

Above left: By late 1932, Preston was finding business hard to get, and the appointment of Mr Walter Luff in November as the new manager of Blackpool Transport Department, who took up his duties from 1 January 1933, set the scene for a revolution in tramcar design. Collaboration with Mr William Lockhart Marshall, the works manager at English Electric, Preston, quickly produced a model of a new single-deck tram mounted on bogies with a streamlined profile. This model was shown by Mr Luff to the Committee on 20 February 1933, and by 20 March 1933 the car works had instructions to build one car for the sum of £2,000. This prototype car was completed and delivered to Blackpool during the evening of 19 June 1933, before being displayed to the Municipal Tramways & Transport Association conference held in Blackpool on 21 June 1933.

In August 1933, English Electric registered the design of the shape of the body and the front profile of the streamlined cars for both Class I and Class III tramcars for a period of five years, registered numbers being 781569 and 781570 respectively.
This first streamline tram, No 200, is seen on the test track at Preston before delivery to Blackpool in June 1933. *EE/Author's collection*

Below left: The production of 24 cars (the railcoaches) followed after an order was placed in August 1933. This time, the price was £2,356 each, 15 being delivered by February 1934. *EE*

Above: A prototype centre-entrance open single-deck car was ordered in November 1933 and delivered in 1934. *EE, courtesy R. Marshall*

Below: A prototype centre-entrance open-top double-deck car, No 226, was also ordered in November 1933. This car was renumbered 237 later in 1934. *R. Elliott*

Above: In early 1931, Mr F. A. Fitzpayne, the General Manager of Edinburgh Corporation Transport, was allocated £4,000 to design and build a new tramcar of lightweight construction capable of carrying more passengers in greater comfort than the existing tramcars used in the city.

In March 1932, Mr Fitzpayne was able to show members of the Scottish Tramways & Transport Association this experimental car, No 180, which had been built by the Corporation in its workshops at Shrubhill. The car had been built using Duralumin for the body framing and as a result, was 5½cwt lighter than earlier type tramcar bodies. By making the sides of the car flat, it had been possible to fit two seats on either side of the gangway in the lower saloon instead of the usual two and one. The resulting seating capacity was 64. Encouraged by this, the Corporation ordered two all-steel tramcar bodies from The Metropolitan & Cammell Carriage Wagon & Finance Co, which completed the two cars, Nos 260 and 265, in early 1933. These seated 62 passengers.

The Corporation, confident that all-steel cars had a future, placed orders in July 1933 with three body-builders for 12 trams similar to No 180. Metropolitan-Cammell-Weymann Motor Bodies Ltd was to build six, and Hurst Nelson & Co Ltd and English Electric Co Ltd were to build three each. The actual design was left to the builder to interpret Mr Fitzpayne's earlier experimental car No 180 as the base model. The English Electric company was the only one to produce a streamline design, where the front sloped backwards from the platform dash. The three EE cars, Nos 262-3 and 267, were delivered in early summer 1934. In December 1934, Edinburgh placed orders for 20 more all-metal tramcars, specifying various changes to the specification based on experience with the earlier cars. This time, Hurst Nelson supplied eight, and Metro-Cammell and English Electric both supplied six. All three manufacturers supplied cars to the style established earlier by English Electric.

The all-metal framework for one of the three cars numbered 262, 263 and 267 is shown here, supplied to Edinburgh in 1934. *EE*

Above right: Car Nos 263-4 were mounted on Maley & Taunton 8ft 0in wheelbase swing link trucks. The semi-streamline profile with domed roof allowed the route number box to be positioned in the front panelling below the top deck window. *EE*

Right: English Electric supplied a new tramcar truck, type FL32 to Edinburgh in late 1932. It was initially used under car number 256, one of the 10 R. Y. Pickering-built cars then being supplied, but was later transferred to car No 267 when this was delivered. *EE*

16
BRAIDS
BRAIDS
263

STANLEY ROAD & BRAIDS
VIA PILRIG STREET
12
KINGS ROAD

Above left: Car No 267 is seen in service mounted on the English Electric type FL32 truck. *EE*

Left: The six English Electric cars built in 1935, numbered 19-24, were externally like the 1934 examples, and, this time, the other two manufacturers adopted the semi-streamline profile.

Edinburgh did not place any further orders for new cars with outside suppliers; instead, between 1934-50, it built a further 83 cars with domed roofs combining the best features from the cars purchased from outside suppliers at its own works. Hurst Nelson obtained orders to build the underframes for the first 46 of these cars.
M. H. Waller, courtesy A. Brotchie collection

Above: For the six cars supplied in 1935 by English Electric, the all-metal framework was modified, with the front lower saloon bulkheads excluded and smaller steel sections used for window rails and other supports. The roof framing was lightened in comparison with the earlier photographs shown. *EE*

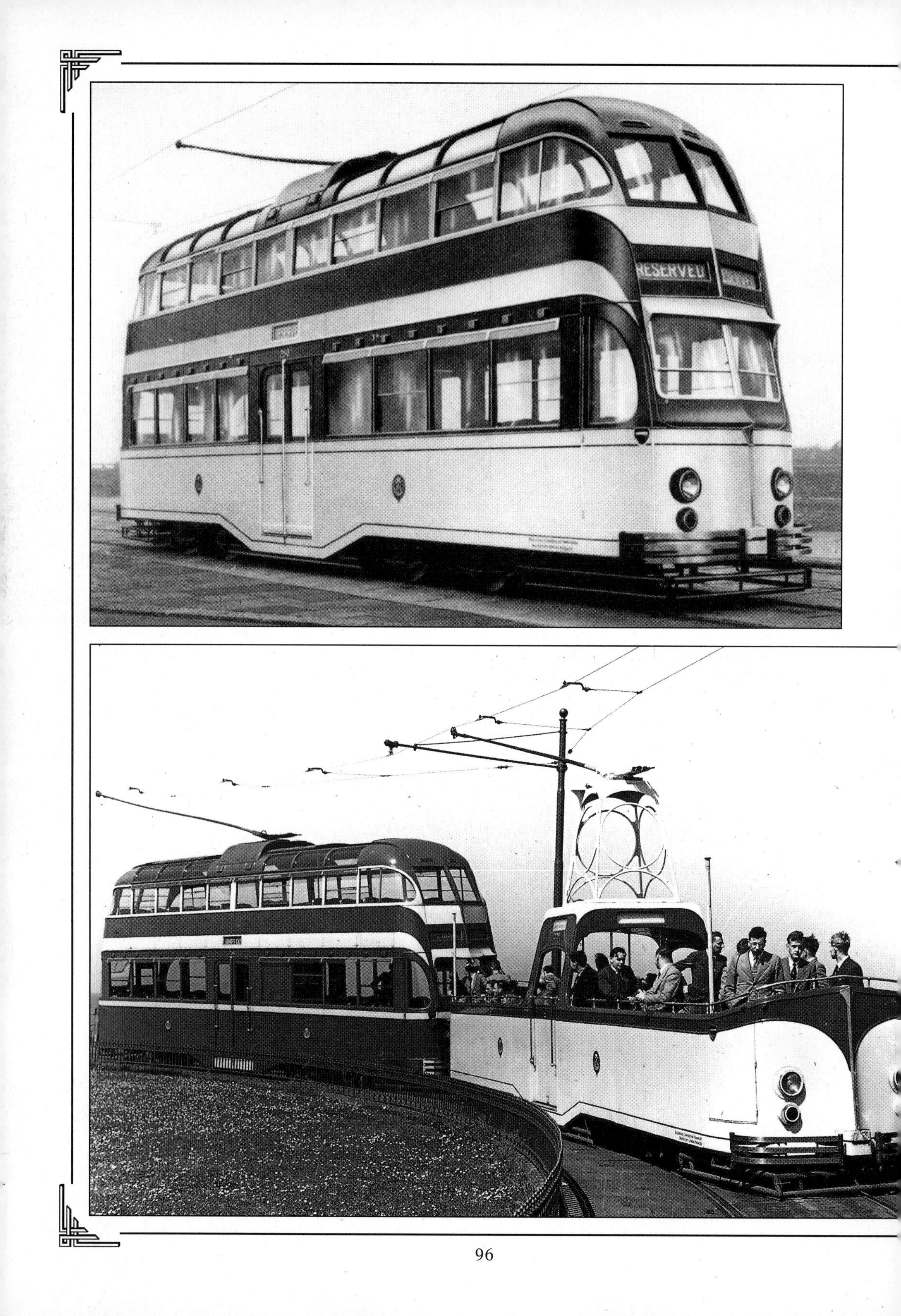
RESERVED

Above left: During January 1934, Blackpool Corporation placed an order for 11 more open 'boat' single-deck centre-entrance cars, this time using equipment salvaged from cars being scrapped. In February 1934, orders for 14 enclosed and 12 open-top double-deck streamlined bogie cars with centre entrances were also placed with English Electric.

All these new cars were 42ft 3in long and were mounted on bogies 19ft 6in apart. The open-top double-deck cars had seating for 94, with 54 on the upper deck on reversible wooden slat seats, whilst the enclosed double-deck cars seated 84, with 44 on upholstered seats on the upper deck. Both types of cars had upholstered seating for 20 provided in each of the two lower saloons. The single-deck boats were similar to the prototype car No 226 ordered in 1933 and delivered in January 1934; the main difference, made for safety reasons, was that the sides of the car were increased in height.

The open boats were given Fleet Nos 226-36, and the open-top double-deck cars Nos 238-49. The earlier prototype open-top double-deck car No 226 was renumbered 237, and the enclosed double-deck cars carried numbers 250-63. The first double-deck enclosed streamline car, No 250, is seen shortly after delivery to Blackpool in 1934. *EE*

Left: No 229, one of the open-boat single-deck cars, is seen at Little Bispham on an enthusiasts' special, while No 258, one of the enclosed double-deck cars, is seen behind, ready to return to Squires Gate. *Roy Brook*

Above: The 12 open-top double-deck cars were, in 1941, fitted with enclosed top covers. On 9 September 1948, one of these rebuilds, car No 246, is seen at the Little Bispham turning circle. These cars were easily recognisable by the different trolley base fitted on the roof. *M. H. Waller*

Sunderland No 99 — Mr Hopkins' Favourite

The General Manager of Sunderland Corporation Tramways, Mr Charles Hopkins, in 1932 was the first choice of Blackpool Transport Committee to replace Mr Charles Furness, who was retiring as Manager of Blackpool Transport Department. However, Sunderland's committee thought otherwise, and Mr Hopkins was persuaded not to take up this new appointment, and instead continue to modernise the Sunderland fleet.

In February 1934, the Corporation ordered a streamlined double-deck centre-entrance bogie car from English Electric. This was 38ft long, cost £2,898 and had seating for 76 passengers — 44 in the upper saloon and 16 in each of the two lower saloons. Two stairways were provided to give access to the upper deck from the centre-entrance vestibule. Like the recently supplied railcoaches and sample toastrack and open-top centre-entrance double-deck car supplied to Blackpool earlier, it was built to a registered design.

The car was fitted with two 4ft 0in wheelbase equal wheel swing axle trucks, each driven by a single longitudinally-mounted 57hp EE305E motor. EE DB1-Z6 controllers were fitted in both end driving compartments, and hand, air-wheel and magnetic brakes were also fitted.

The first photograph *(above left)* shows the car mounted on the MRS transporter, ready to leave the Preston works. At this point, it is carrying the Sunderland coat of arms above only the centre entrance. By the time it entered service on 22 August 1934, it had gained fleet No 99 and had two coats of arms on diamonds, instead of the original one. The other two photographs *(left and above)* show No 99 on the front at Seaburn. *EE*

Above and below: In December 1933, Rotherham Corporation invited tenders for the supply of six tramcar bodies and trucks. English Electric was chosen in February 1934 to supply six bodies for the sum of £9,417 suitable for mounting on EMB-supplied flexible axle 4wheel trucks equipped with both air and magnetic brakes.

These tramcars were designed by Mr T. P. Sykes, the General Manager of the Transport Department, and were being purchased for use on the jointly operated service to Sheffield, which, to speed up turnround, had terminal loops at each end of the route. They were built as single-ended cars which resembled contemporary modern trolleybus bodies mounted on a tramcar truck. The car bodies were 29ft 3in long and 7ft 1in wide, with all 63 seats facing forward, 36 in the upper and 27 in the lower saloons. In March 1934, English Electric, jointly with Tom Percy Sykes, patented the design (Patent No 422091).

Delivery of these six cars commenced in August 1934, and progressively during October they were put into service on the Sheffield route. The public reaction to them was such that Rotherham's share of passengers on the route increased by 12%. One of the cars was displayed at the Preston works in the first week of December 1934, when English Electric held a 'Little Olympia' exhibition for the industry. Rotherham had completed the final assembly of these tramcars, fitting two 40hp GEC motors, GEC type TE5/R1Z controllers in the front driving cab, and in the rear driving cab, a Dick, Kerr DB1 controller. This was to allow the car to be moved in the depot or reversed at triangular junctions at Templeborough or in Sheffield's Tinsley depot if they were used for short workings.

All this equipment had been recovered from tramcars scrapped earlier; hence the cars were underpowered when compared to the Sheffield cars used on the service which had two 50hp motors.

The two photographs show car No 1 on the test track at Preston before dispatch in August 1934 to Rotherham. *EE*

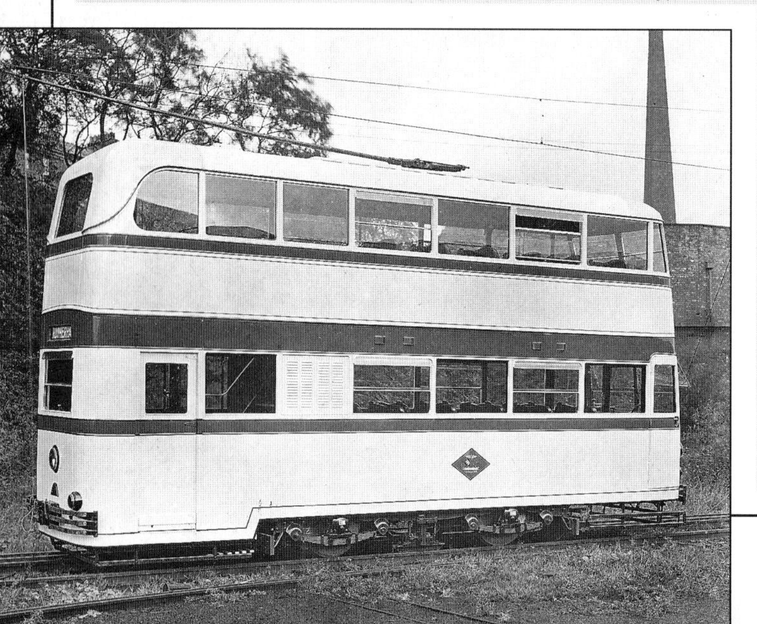

Above right: In January 1932, Mr W. Vane Morland was selected to be the new General Manager of the Leeds City Tramways & Transport Department. Mr Morland, an advocate of modern methods of transport, saw the need to continue the modernisation of the tramways as the most efficient means of moving the bulk of the city's population.

For use on the Middleton Light Railway, linking the extensive new housing estate at Middleton with the city where the reserved sleeper track for part of the route enabled fast schedules to be maintained, he persuaded the council to purchase a prototype tramcar designed on modern lines and built to his specification. Brush Electrical Engineering Co Ltd of Loughborough built this prototype car No 255 which entered service in May 1933 for prolonged trials, having cost approximately £3,000 to develop and build.

Satisfied with this car, a further 16 cars were sanctioned by the Council in February 1934. This time, the order for the bodies was split between Brush and English Electric. Each of the eight English Electric-built bodies cost £1,219 4s 2d, 17% cheaper than the eight Brush-built ones which each cost £1,470 12s 9d.

Leeds ordered the 32 bogie trucks from Maley & Taunton Ltd of Wednesbury, with GEC Ltd supplying the four 40hp WT181A tramway motors for each of the 16 cars, and finally, Metropolitan Vickers Electrical Co Ltd supplying the necessary control equipments. The final cost to Leeds was £2,589 10s 6d for the English Electric-bodied cars and £2,840 19s 1d for the ones with Brush bodies.

In view of the difficulties that English Electric Co was experiencing during the 1930s' depression, this price difference gives support to the statements that 'the company was prepared to undertake work at cost in an attempt to keep the works open'.

Unlike the prototype car No 255, which had the staircase on the offside, these modern-looking cars were fitted with straight staircases installed on the nearside adjacent to the entrances. Accommodation for 70 seated passengers was achieved by fitting 40 seats in the upper saloon and 30 seats in the lower saloon. The cars were all built to the same specification, although minor differences, such as the type of ventilators used by the builders, could be found. The cars were 35ft 6in long, 6ft 11in wide and were of composite construction, using Burma teak framing, metal flitches etc, and each car weighed 16 tons. The headlights fitted to both ends were mounted 4ft 8½in apart to enable them to illuminate the rails in front of the car on the separate sleeper track right of way through Middleton Woods.

One of these cars was displayed at the 'Little Olympia' show held at the Preston works in early December 1934. The EE cars were given numbers 264-71, and after delivery to Leeds in two sections, they were reassembled at the Kirkstall Road works, entering service between February and April 1935.

Duncan Street, Briggate, Leeds, is the backdrop for this prewar animated city street scene featuring centre stage Middleton bogie No 269 in original style livery and sporting Gill Sans numerals. *W. B. Stocks/Author's collection*

Above: Car No 265 in early postwar livery speeds through Middleton Woods on the superb two-mile-long private right of way. The trackbed of this magnificent tramway, abandoned in 1959, is now a woodland public footpath. *MV/Author's collection*

4 Financial Problems – Restructuring

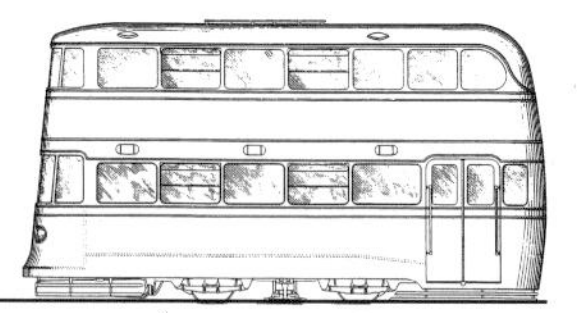

From 1918 until 1926 parts of the new English Electric group of companies continued to design and build aircraft, specialising in flying boats. The design team was based at the Phoenix Works at Bradford, but production ceased due to lack of orders.

In the three years 1926, 1927 and 1928, the EE group made trading losses of £123,000; £134,000 and £33,000 respectively. In 1927, Mr W. L. Hitchens was appointed Chairman, and began reorganising the company, initially by reducing the fixed charges. This included the closure of non-viable works. In early 1930 the shareholders of the English Electric company agreed to write down the existing capital by £1,755,000. This meant that six £1 Ordinary shares were now revalued as one new £1 Ordinary share. The company was also refinanced by the injection of £750,000 from Lazard Brothers & Co Ltd, who also asked for the resignation of three directors so that four of their nominees could serve on the Board. These nominees were Mr F. Massingberd Rogers (Greater London & Counties Trust), Sir Edward Hilton Young PC, MP, Mr Percy Horsfall (Lazard Brothers & Co Ltd) and Col Wade Hampton Hayes (Chase Securities Corporation). The three directors who resigned were Sir Charles E. Ellis, Sir John A. F. Aspinall and Col Sir John M. Mansell. In late July 1930, Mr W. L. Hitchens, having resigned his position as Chairman, retired from the Board and Sir Holberry Mensforth KCB, CBE was elected to the Board and appointed the new Chairman of the company.

The next change occurred in October 1930 when Mr Victor Watlington relinquished his position as Managing Director, but continued to be a Director. This move allowed recently appointed director Mr George H. Nelson to take up the duties of Managing Director and try to reorganise the company and revitalise its activities. Because of these changes, by the end of 1930 only three of the original 1919 directors were still on the Board.

The changes introduced by Mr W. L. Hitchens were now taking effect. The manufacture of traction equipment was transferred to Bradford, and by late 1930 the large West Works were empty and lay unused until the Car Works production was moved into them in 1938.

In February 1930, Mr R. von Zweigbergh died. Despite his retirement as Technical Director of Dick, Kerr & Co Ltd in 1920, he had continued in the capacity of consulting engineer to the English Electric Company. He had been recently involved in the design of the Monomotor bogie for Liverpool, and his death meant that English Electric had difficulties in resolving teething troubles when the first production Monomotor bogies entered service in 1931. Shortly after his death, the English Electric Company entered into an agreement with Westinghouse Electric & Manufacturing Co of East Pittsburg and the Westinghouse Electric International Company of New York for the exchange of technical information on steam turbines and electrical apparatus. This agreement allowed access to research facilities which the company had been unable to fund in preceding years. In exchange, Westinghouse was offered a small percentage of ordinary shares.

Mr George H. Nelson became Managing Director of English Electric in late 1930 following many years of responsible positions and came with a background in electrical engineering. He and the recently appointed Chairman, Sir Holberry Mensforth, reorganised the management and manufacturing facilities. Production was now concentrated at Rugby, Bradford and Stafford, with the exception being the manufacture of rolling stock and bus bodies at Preston. Stafford was also chosen to be the main base for the company's activities, with research facilities also being established there.

In May 1933, Lord Meston resigned from the Board and was replaced by Sir Gerald F. Talbot. In July 1933, G. H. Nelson was appointed Chairman of the Board in addition

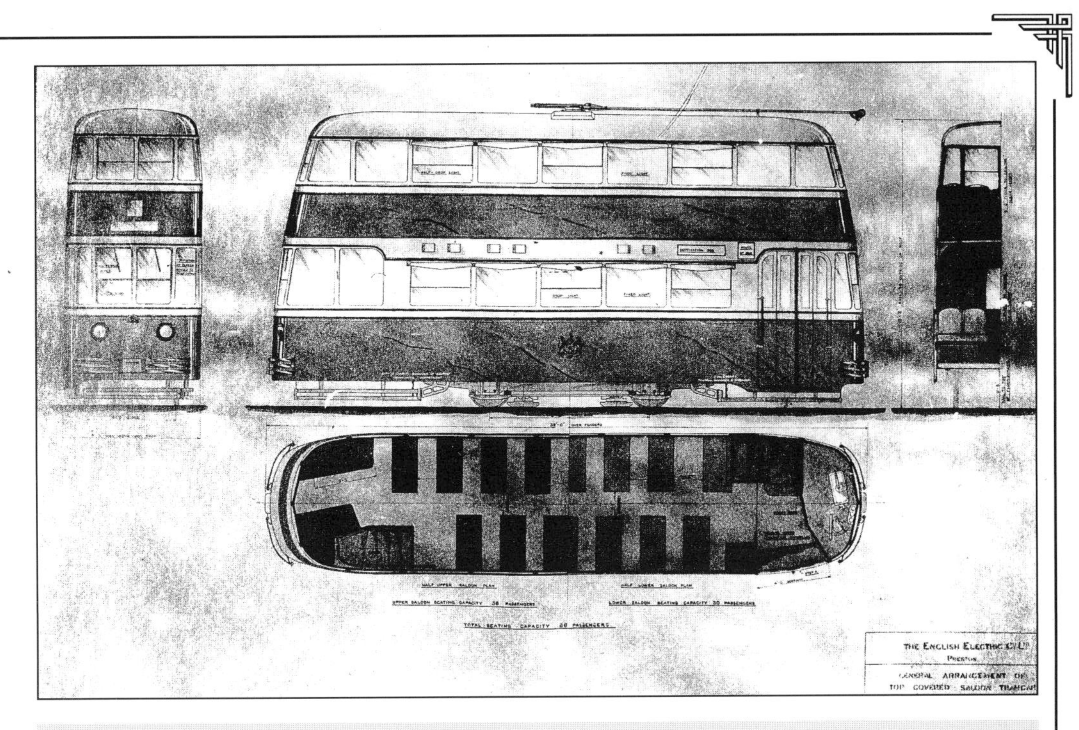

Above: On 1 January 1934, Belfast City Council approved the purchase of 50 new tramcars, which were expected to cost £2,400 each. After obtaining sanction from the Ministry of Home Affairs to borrow the necessary £120,000, the Council in late February invited tenders for the supply of:

- 50 tramcar bodies
- 50 tramcar trucks including wheels and axles
- 50 tramcar electrical equipment and spares.

At the end of May 1934, the Tramways Committee accepted the design submitted by the English Electric Co Ltd, placing an order with them for 20 bodies. A further 20 bodies of composite construction in the same design were ordered from Service Motor Works Ltd, Belfast. The remaining 10 were to be supplied with all-metal bodies by Metropolitan-Cammell-Weymann Motor Bodies Ltd. The Committee specified that in each case a sample car must be built and that work on the remaining cars had not to proceed until the General Manager, Major McCreary, had certified that the car was built to the specification and was acceptable to him.

The order for the tramcar trucks was placed with Maley & Taunton for 8ft 0in wheelbase swing-link trucks. The remaining order for the electrical equipment was placed with Crompton-Parkinson and included two 50hp self-ventilating motors.

At the end of January 1935, the Tramways Committee was informed by the General Manager that the tender for the 10 all-metal tramcar bodies was substantially in excess of the cost of composite cars already on order. The Committee decided then not to proceed with the purchase of the all-metal bodies and, subject to approval, arranged for the placing of an order for 10 additional composite bodies with Service Motor Works, Belfast.

The sample cars built by EE (No 392) and SMW (No 393) entered service in April 1935 and immediately created much interest with the travelling public. Their modern streamlined appearance was enhanced by the curved stainless steel collision fenders fitted to both ends of the 32ft 0in-long car. The timber-framed body, suitably strengthened by metal flitching and angle brackets, was mounted on a steel underframe. The floor of the lower saloon sloped down to the end platforms, avoiding the step usually found on other cars. The cars had seating provided for 64 passengers, 40 in the upper saloon on double transverse seats, whilst in the lower saloon accommodation was provided for 24, comprising two longitudinal bench seats for three passengers at each end of the saloon, and four rows of double and single transverse seats in the middle.

Satisfied with the sample cars, instructions were given to complete the other cars. These incorporated various minor differences to the two sample cars, which for example had been provided with separate driving cabs, all the cars having patent Maley & Taunton air brake equipment comprising air track, air-wheel and magnetic track brakes. The remainder of the SMW built cars were numbered 394-422 and the EE-built cars 423-41. *Caption continued on page104.*

Caption continued from page103.

The EE-built cars could be easily recognised by the front headlights which were positioned considerably higher than those built by SMW. The EE cars were also the first tramcars to be built with illuminated direction arrows operated by the motorman to advise other road users which way the tramcar was proceeding at road junctions. The use of these anticipated by 30 years the introduction of flashing direction indicators on all road vehicles.

English Electric drawing No PC34/136 shows the original design submitted to Belfast in 1934, and its frontal appearance is similar to the earlier Rotherham and later Aberdeen tramcars. *EE*

Right: Belfast No 392, the sample car built by English Electric, was photographed on 11 April 1935 by the Belfast photographer A. R. Hogg. *A. Montgomery*

to his responsibilities as Managing Director, despite the record losses and the value of the shares falling from £1 to 6s 3d.

Below: One of the 19 production tramcar bodies which followed shows a number of variations in detail, such as lack of wind shields above some windows. *EE*

Left: The front view of the same body shows the driver's nearside mirror and the illuminated direction arrows. *EE*

Below: In March 1935, to enable Rotherham Corporation to use only single-ended cars on the Sheffield service, orders were placed with English Electric for a further five 63-seat car bodies similar to the previous six. Once again, EMB obtained the order for the hornless trucks with air-wheel and magnetic track brakes. This time, Rotherham purchased new electrical equipment from GEC comprising WT294B motors and type KH/7 controllers which were fitted to both ends.

These five new cars arrived in Rotherham during August and September 1935 and, like the previous six cars, the lower saloon was fitted with luggage racks whilst the floors of both saloons were covered in linoleum. The straight staircase was easy to use and the cars were provided with thermostatically-controlled electric heating. The 63 passengers were all seated on forward facing seats comparable to contemporary motorbuses, with 36 seated upstairs and 27 in the lower saloon. *EE*

Below right: In late December 1934, Blackpool Corporation placed an order with English Electric for the supply of a further 20 single-deck 'railcoaches' with centre entrances, similar to the 24 supplied in 1933-4. This time they were mounted on equal wheel swing axle bogies with a wheelbase of 4ft 9in. The electrical equipment comprised two EE305E 57hp motors and DB1-Z6 controllers. The cars, numbered 264-83, were ordered as 50-seaters, 48 in the two saloons and presumably two tip-up seats in the centre entrance vestibule. Delivery commenced in June 1935. Car No 273 is seen at Squires Gate on 9 September 1948 in the predominantly green livery introduced during the war. *M. H. Waller*

On 18 November 1935, Darwen Corporation Tramways placed an order with English Electric for the supply of two double-deck streamline tramcars for the sum of £2,750 each. In the EE press release in February 1936, it was stated that 'these will follow closely the lines of the new streamline railcoaches recently supplied to Blackpool. They will be of the centre-entrance type, provided with all the latest improvements fitted on modern rolling stock.'

The first one was placed into service in mid-June 1936 on the 'main line' between Whitehall, Darwen and Blackburn, a route which was operated jointly with Blackburn Corporation. It proved to be an instant success with the travelling public, and the two cars became known as the 'Queen Marys' after the transatlantic liner.

These two cars, Nos 23 and 24 in the Darwen fleet, were a narrow gauge version of Sunderland car No 99, the principal dimensions being: length 35ft 6in, width 6ft 7½in and height to trolley plank 14ft 8in. A pair of 4ft gauge EE maximum traction bogie trucks with a wheelbase of 4ft 6in were provided with 27in diameter wheels on the driven axles and 21in diameter pony wheels on the other axles. Each truck was powered by a 57hp EE type 305A motor. EE type DB1-K33E controllers were fitted in each of the two driving compartments. The cars were fitted with hand brake, air brakes and air hooters.

The body framing was in teak with intermediate pillars bracketed and flitch plated to the body structure for rigidity. The staircases were immediately to the left of the central entrance and exit, which had folding platforms doors. When ordered, the specification called for 52 reversible Dunlopillo cushion seats, the upper saloons having 12 double reversible seats, two double fixed seats with their backs against the staircases and four single reversible seats. The lower saloons each had two double and two single reversible seats, all facing forward, and a bench seat for four passengers facing the staircase. At some date, it appears that the lower saloons were modified to seat 12, raising the seating capacity to 56.

The two cars were withdrawn from service by 1945. They were the only EE streamlined cars to be resold for further use, being purchased by Llandudno & Colwyn Bay Electric Railway for £400 each in 1946, after regauging the trucks to suit the L&CB 3ft 6in gauge tracks. They entered service in April 1948, being restricted for use only on the shuttle services operated in either Llandudno or Colwyn Bay. When travelling to Llandudno from the depot, they were not allowed to carry passengers on the exposed sections between the Rhos depot and Craig-y-don. By the early 1950s this restriction caused the cars to be used only occasionally, and by 1954 they were officially withdrawn. Incidentally, they also carried fleet numbers 23 and 24 at Llandudno & Colwyn Bay, with Darwen No 24 becoming L&CB No 23 and vice versa.

Left: Car No 23 is seen on the main line near Blackburn Boundary in June 1936. *EE*

Right: Timber-framed lower deck of one of the cars, with the upper deck being built behind it. *EE*

Centre right: The EE maximum traction truck showing framing, 57hp motor, brake gear and both driving and pony axles. *EE*

Below left: Interior view of the lower saloon. *EE*

Below right: Interior view of the upper saloon showing the 2 & 1 seating layout. *EE*

Over leaf:
The limitations on the width of the car caused by the narrow gauge of 4ft are clearly shown in this view of No 23. Compare this with the view of Sunderland No 99 on page 99. *EE*

DARWEN
WHITEHALL

Above: The introduction of Luxury Car No 99 at Sunderland with its wide central entrance and low entrance steps for passengers, was a design easily accommodated on a bogie car. However, it was not suitable for use on routes with sharp curves and limited clearances between rail and kerb where the risk of accidents was high, since the centre entrance was proving to be a success in reducing boarding accidents. Charles Hopkins persuaded Maley & Taunton Ltd, to design a new type of single truck with a cranked frame working closely with Brush Electrical Engineering Co Ltd. The first single truck centre-entrance tramcar was delivered to Sunderland in December 1935. Another one followed in April 1936, being built by Sunderland on a steel underframe and body shell supplied by Brush. In December 1935, Sunderland ordered a similar type of car from English Electric, who supplied a type FL32 9ft wheelbase drop centre truck, mechanical equipment, the steel underframe, the car body framing and type DB1-Z4 controllers. Sunderland supplied two GEC WT28 50hp motors and completed the assembly of the car, and the total cost was £2,795 by the time the car entered service in December 1936. This time, the staircase was immediately to the left of the 3ft 9in-wide centre entrance, which had a sliding door. The car was 32ft long and in appearance was a smaller version of car No 99, Mr Hopkins' favourite tramcar.

Depicted is a view of the EE type FL32 9ft wheelbase drop centre truck built for Sunderland 53. *EE*

Below: Sunderland car No 53 is seen at Roker in early 1937. *EE*

After trials with two experimental cars, Nos 1141 and 1142, in February 1937 Glasgow Corporation approved the building of 100 new tramcars at the Coplawhill works of the Transport Department. Tenders for the supply of bogies and electrical equipment were accepted and orders were placed with the Electro-Mechanical Brake Company Ltd of West Bromwich and British Thomson-Houston Ltd of Rugby respectively. The manufacture of the fabricated steel underframes and lower saloon body framing was subcontracted to English Electric Co for manufacture at Preston. Glasgow then completed the manufacture in its works, fitting upper decks and interior fittings, as well as the mechanical and electrical equipment.

Above left: One of the all-welded subframes is seen waiting in the West Works yard before departure by rail to Glasgow. *EE*

Below left: One of the first cars to be completed by Glasgow was car No 1146, which was photographed in early December 1937 on a test run. During December 1938, English Electric received orders for a further 50 all-welded tramcar underframes and lower saloon framing. The two batches of tramcars, Glasgow Nos 1143-292, were known as Coronation Mark 1 cars. *BTH/Author's collection*

Right: In January 1939, Blackpool Corporation accepted the tender submitted by English Electric for the supply of 12 semi-open railcoaches with centre entrances. This time the cars had 4ft 3in wheelbase equal wheel bogies and the electrical equipment comprised refurbished BTH 265C motors and new DB1-K53E controllers. The car bodies were fitted with wooden seats for 56 passengers and were devoid of partitions between passengers and the driver. The entrance doors were only waist high, and only the bottom half of the windows had glazing. A folding canvas cover was used to cover the open roof in bad weather. The cars, numbered 10-21, were delivered between August and October 1939, but with the outbreak of war in September 1939, they were little used and in 1941 special permission was obtained to enclose the cars and fit partitions, this being done in 1942.

In 1948-51, the cars were reseated to 48 and used to replace double-deck cars on the Marton route, and between 1949-52 they were fitted with the new M&T HS44 bogies and new electrical equipment comprising Crompton-Parkinson motors and Vambac control equipment.

Car No 10 is seen at Talbot Square, Blackpool, waiting to return by the Royal Oak via Marton in 1947 prior to fitting the new electrical equipment. *Roy Brook*

Below: Two of the cars fitted with Vambac control equipment are seen at Royal Oak, the control gear accelerator being housed in the base of the trolley tower. *Author*

Above: Once Sunderland had placed English Electric-supplied car No 53 into service in December 1936, it was able to compare it with the two built earlier by Brush. The outcome was the placing of orders for the supply of three sets of components for Sunderland to assemble in its own workshops.

English Electric supplied three underframes and body shells for centre-entrance streamlined cars to be built to its registered design. They also supplied the 9ft wheelbase cranked truck of the flexible suspension type. The electrical equipment comprised Crompton-Parkinson 62hp motors and English Electric DB1-Z4 controllers. The magnetic brakes were also supplied by EE, whilst Maley & Taunton supplied the air brakes.

The three cars, numbered 49-51, entered service between May and July 1938. In April 1939, a fourth car was sanctioned and built using a further kit of parts. This car, No 52, entered service in May 1940. These cars cost approximately £2,800 to build, and car No 52 was the last double-deck tramcar to be built to the English Electric-registered design. It was also the last new car to be built by Sunderland. Car No 51 is seen here in April 1952 working the Circle route. *Roy Marshall*

Left: Car No 53, and 0one of the last four, shows the minor differences in these cars: rainshields, rear lights, etc. *A. D. Packer*

Right: In early 1939, the General Manager of Aberdeen Corporation Tramways, Mr Alfred Smith, prepared a comprehensive report for the Transport Committee suggesting various ways of modernising the Granite City's tramway system. Amongst these was the purchase of a number of new tramcars. On 26 June 1939, the Committee, accepting the report, agreed to purchase two single-truck tramcars and two equal wheel bogie tramcars, the latter having central entrances and dual stair-cases, these four to be tried in service to establish which was the most suitable type for the city. Orders were placed with EMB Co Ltd of West Bromwich for the supply of two hornless fourwheel trucks, type A0, costing £480 each, and two sets of 4ft 9in wheelbase type LS lightweight bogies, costing £599 per set. These were to be delivered to Preston where the motors would be fitted. English Electric had obtained the order for the traction motors, control equipment and tramcar bodies, which cost £3,100 each for the two four-wheel cars and £3,240 each for the two bogie cars.

The four cars were built in the West Works at Preston, which after standing empty for eight years, had been refurbished to allow production of road vehicle bodies, complete tramcars, railway rolling stock and locomotives to be undertaken using modern methods. By 1939, the former car works, the East Works, had been adapted to produce Handley Page aircraft for the Air Ministry due to the national emergency. Although World War 2 had started in September 1939, the four cars were completed and delivered to Aberdeen during July and August 1940, the bogie cars being numbered 138 and 139, and the single-truck cars 140 and 141.

Aberdeen, after evaluating both types, decided to order a fleet of 20 bogie cars to complete the modernisation of its system, but had to wait until 2 September 1946 before it could place orders for these with English Electric and EMB. The order placed with English Electric was for a further 20 equal wheel bogie tramcars; this time the price quoted was £6,946 each, and delivery was to commence in 14 months at the rate of three per month. The order placed with EMB was for a modified version of the original type L5 lightweight bogies, this time with a 5ft 0in wheelbase costing £1,650 per set.

Because of problems in returning factories to civilian production after the war, both English Electric and EMB found it necessary to subcontract work previously done in their own works. English Electric chose to subcontract the manufacture of the fabricated underframe and the bodywork to R. Y. Pickering & Co at Wishaw in Scotland.

EMB had arranged for M. B. Wild & Co Ltd to manufacture tramcar trucks on their behalf since their own works were fully occupied with more profitable work. By the time the order was completed in 1949, prices had escalated so that the bodies and electrical equipment cost £8,451 each, whilst the trucks cost £2,901 2s 0d per set, a considerable increase on the 1946 quoted prices. The final cost of these new cars was £11,358 2s 0d, each three times the cost of the 1940 experimental bogie car.

The bogie cars supplied to Aberdeen were 38ft 0in long, 7ft 1¾in wide. The 4ft 6in-wide entrance had the platform height 1ft 4in above the rails, with straight staircases immediately to the right side of the entrance. The seating capacity was arranged to accommodate 16 in each of the two lower saloons and 44 in the upper saloon. The teak-framed body with necessary metal flitches was mounted on a fabricated steel underframe constructed from rolled steel channels, angles and steel plates, which was welded together to give a substantial frame suitable for heavy duty service.

The EMB bogies were each fitted with two 34hp EE type 327 motors with the air-wheel, air track and magnetic brakes fitted with the EMB patent interlock control system to give maximum braking effort without wheel skid.

The two single truck cars were 32ft 0in long, 7ft 1¾in wide and were similar in appearance to the bogie cars, but with the passenger entrances at the ends. The seating capacity was 64, and a 90° turn staircase was fitted giving access to the upper saloon from the platforms. Again, the body was teak-framed with metal stiffeners, mounted on a substantial fabricated steel frame. The 8ft 6in wheelbase EMB swing axle four-wheel hornless truck was fitted with two motor equipments comprising 57hp EE type 305 motors and similar braking and electrical equipment to the bogie cars. These cars represented the ultimate English Electric tramcar design for a British operator.

This photograph of the lower saloon body framing for the Aberdeen bogie car shows clearly the teak frame with temporary cross-bracing fitted while the upper deck floor framing was being constructed. *EE*

Left: A similarly cross-braced upper saloon body framing partially built and waiting for panelling to be fitted. *EE*

Centre left: One of the EMB 4ft 9in wheelbase type LS equal wheel bogies at Preston before the EE traction motors were fitted. *EE*

Below: One of the EMB 8ft 6in wheelbase type AO swing axle trucks, again prior to fitting the EE traction motors. *EE*

Left: Aberdeen car No 138 is seen in July 1940 after delivery, posed for the photographer on a damp day while the people in the background watch and wonder what all the fuss is about. *EE*

Right: Aberdeen car No 138 was also photographed later in the day. This is the full side view complete with reflections on the wet road. *EE*

Below: Interior of one of the bogie cars showing curved quarterlights. *EE*

Centre right: Interior of one of the bogie cars showing the extremely high standard of interior decor, concealed lighting and upholstered seats in the lower saloon. *EE*

Right: Aberdeen single-truck car No 140 is seen in July 1940 outside Mannofield depot. *EE*

Probably when Aberdeen car No 141 was photographed in the West Works in 1940, nobody realised that this would be the last tramcar to be built at Preston. The changes in the company's activities brought about by the war meant that the next order had the bodywork subcontracted elsewhere. *EE*

Appendices

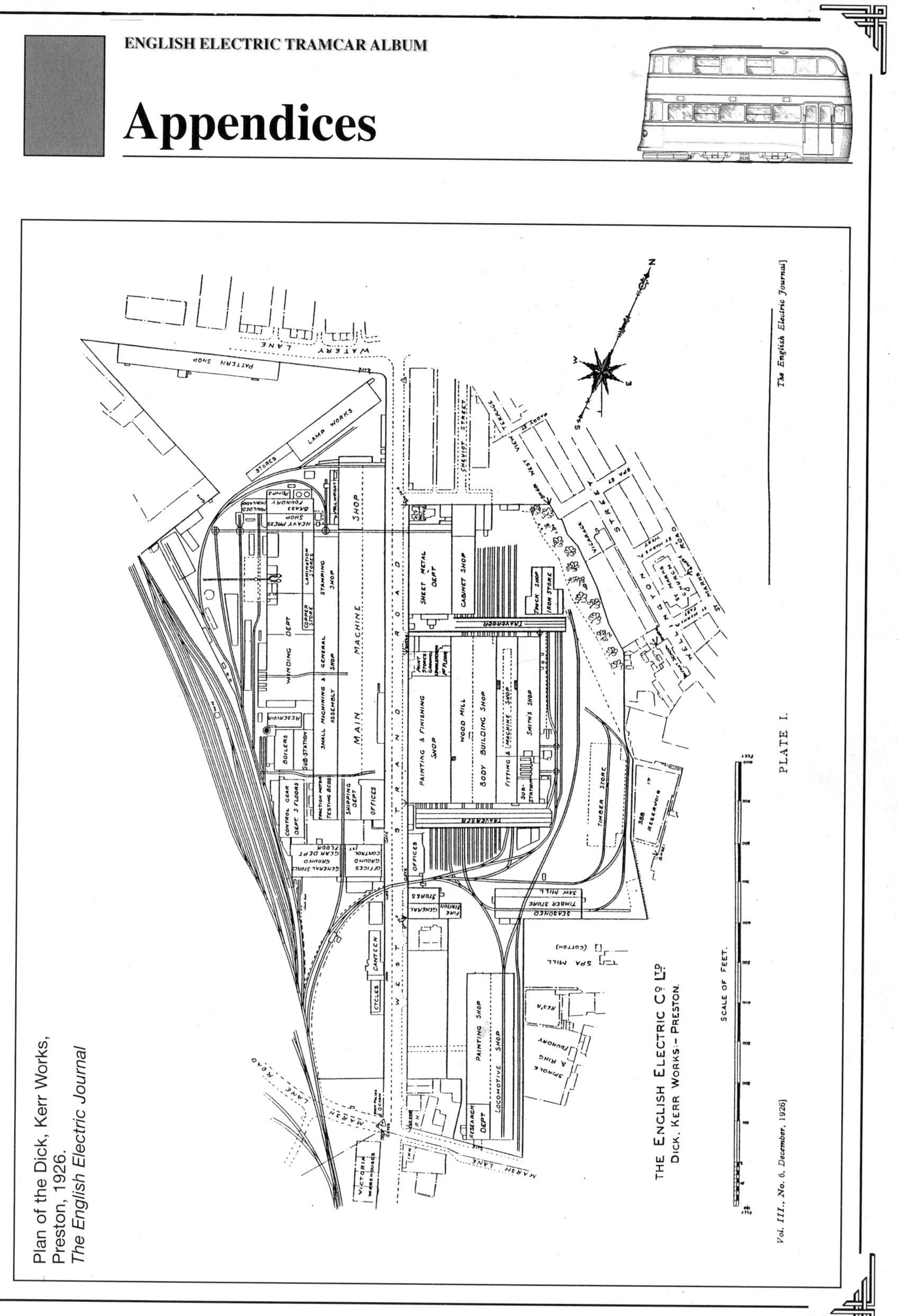

Plan of the Dick, Kerr Works, Preston, 1926.
The English Electric Journal

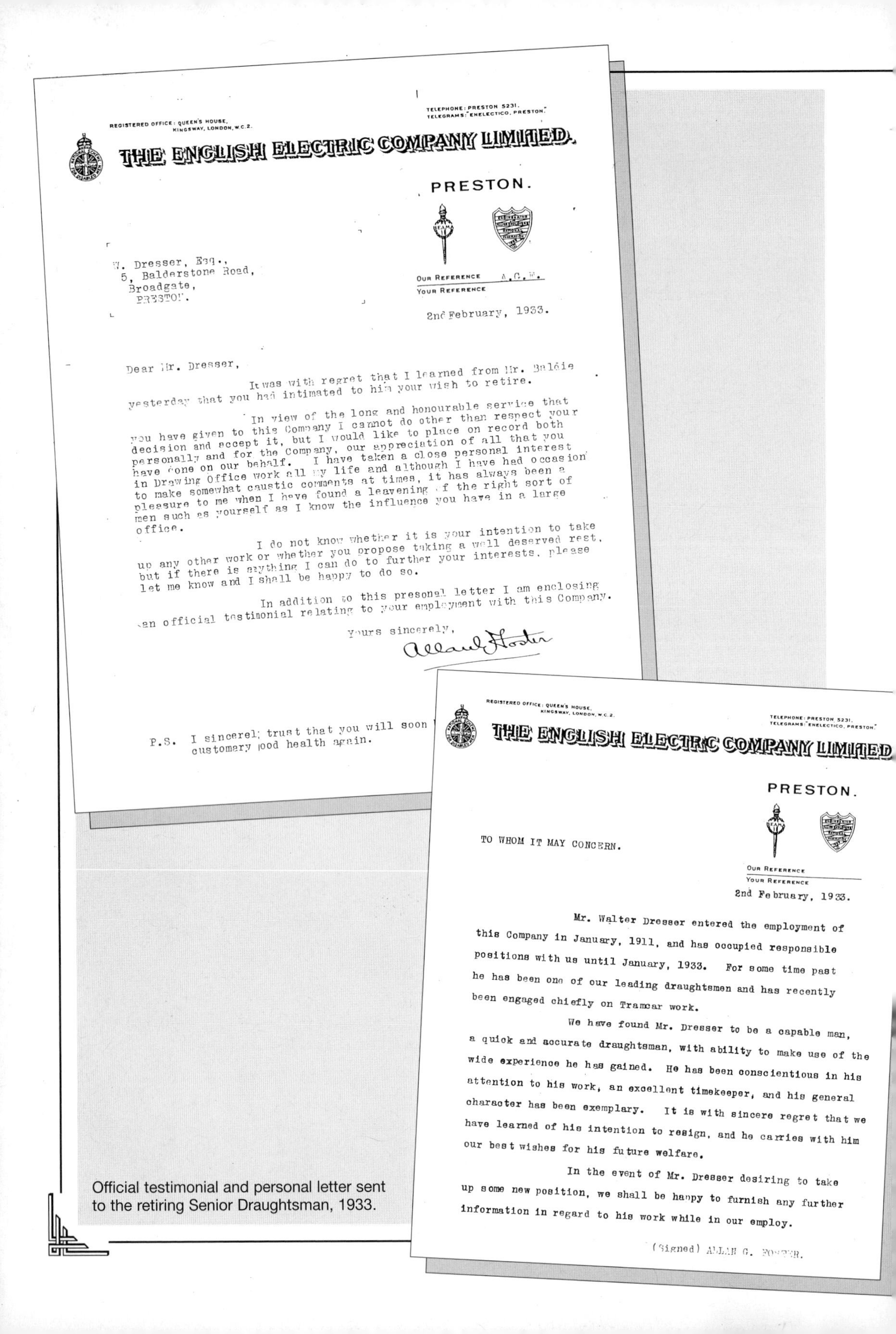
REGISTERED OFFICE: QUEEN'S HOUSE, KINGSWAY, LONDON, W.C.2.

TELEPHONE: PRESTON 5231.
TELEGRAMS: "ENELECTICO, PRESTON."

THE ENGLISH ELECTRIC COMPANY LIMITED.

PRESTON.

W. Dresser, Esq.,
5, Balderstone Road,
Broadgate,
PRESTON.

OUR REFERENCE A.G.F.
YOUR REFERENCE

2nd February, 1933.

Dear Mr. Dresser,

It was with regret that I learned from Mr. Baldie yesterday that you had intimated to him your wish to retire.

In view of the long and honourable service that you have given to this Company I cannot do other than respect your decision and accept it, but I would like to place on record both personally and for the Company, our appreciation of all that you have done on our behalf. I have taken a close personal interest in Drawing Office work all my life and although I have had occasion to make somewhat caustic comments at times, it has always been a pleasure to me when I have found a leavening of the right sort of men such as yourself as I know the influence you have in a large office.

I do not know whether it is your intention to take up any other work or whether you propose taking a well deserved rest, but if there is anything I can do to further your interests, please let me know and I shall be happy to do so.

In addition to this presonal letter I am enclosing an official testimonial relating to your employment with this Company.

Yours sincerely,

Allan G. Foster

P.S. I sincerely trust that you will soon [...] customary good health again.

REGISTERED OFFICE: QUEEN'S HOUSE, KINGSWAY, LONDON, W.C.2.

TELEPHONE: PRESTON 5231.
TELEGRAMS: "ENELECTICO, PRESTON."

THE ENGLISH ELECTRIC COMPANY LIMITED

PRESTON.

TO WHOM IT MAY CONCERN.

OUR REFERENCE
YOUR REFERENCE

2nd February, 1933.

Mr. Walter Dresser entered the employment of this Company in January, 1911, and has occupied responsible positions with us until January, 1933. For some time past he has been one of our leading draughtsmen and has recently been engaged chiefly on Tramcar work.

We have found Mr. Dresser to be a capable man, a quick and accurate draughtsman, with ability to make use of the wide experience he has gained. He has been conscientious in his attention to his work, an excellent timekeeper, and his general character has been exemplary. It is with sincere regret that we have learned of his intention to resign, and he carries with him our best wishes for his future welfare.

In the event of Mr. Dresser desiring to take up some new position, we shall be happy to furnish any further information in regard to his work while in our employ.

(Signed) ALLAN G. FOSTER.

Official testimonial and personal letter sent to the retiring Senior Draughtsman, 1933.

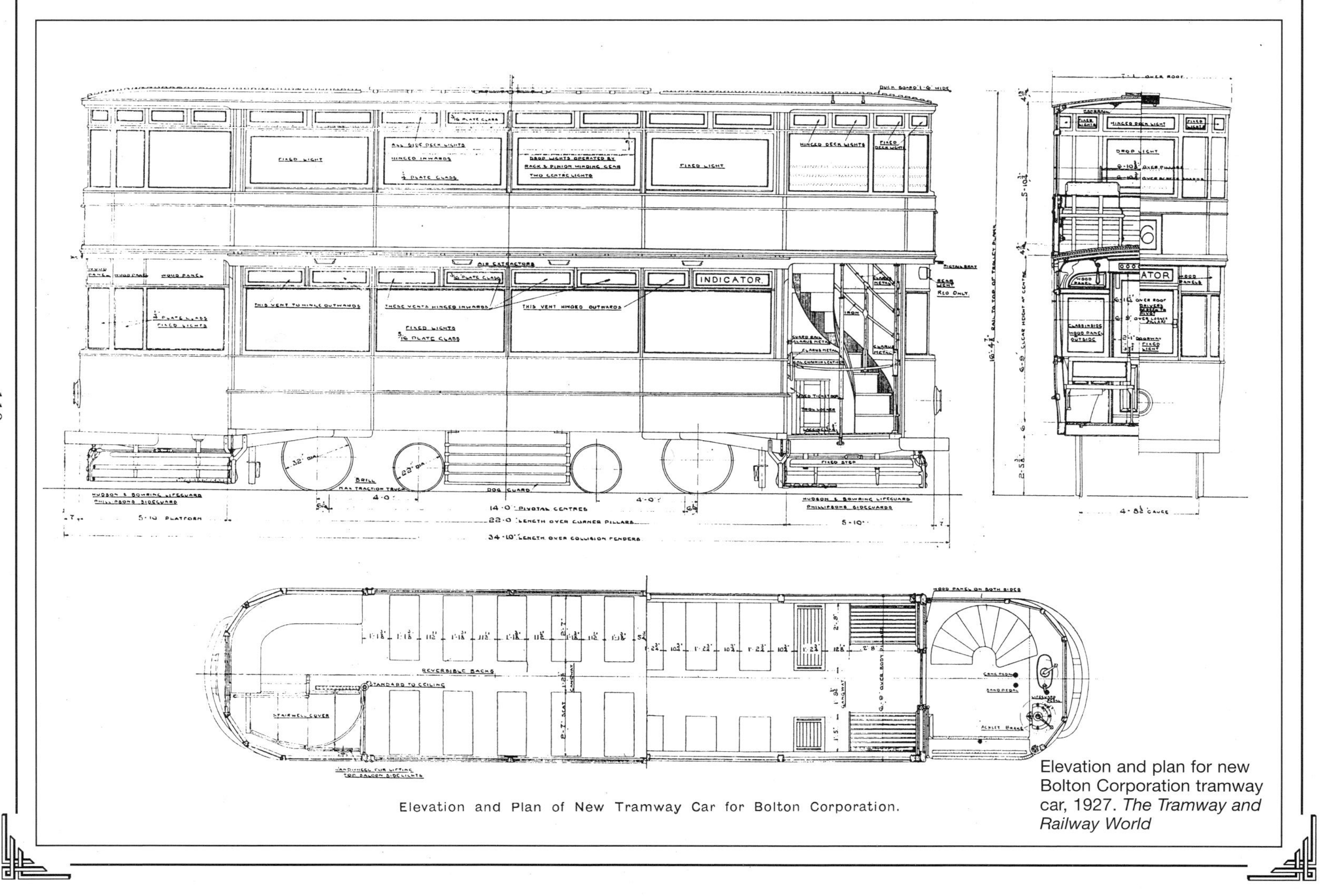

Elevation and Plan of New Tramway Car for Bolton Corporation.

Elevation and plan for new Bolton Corporation tramway car, 1927. *The Tramway and Railway World*

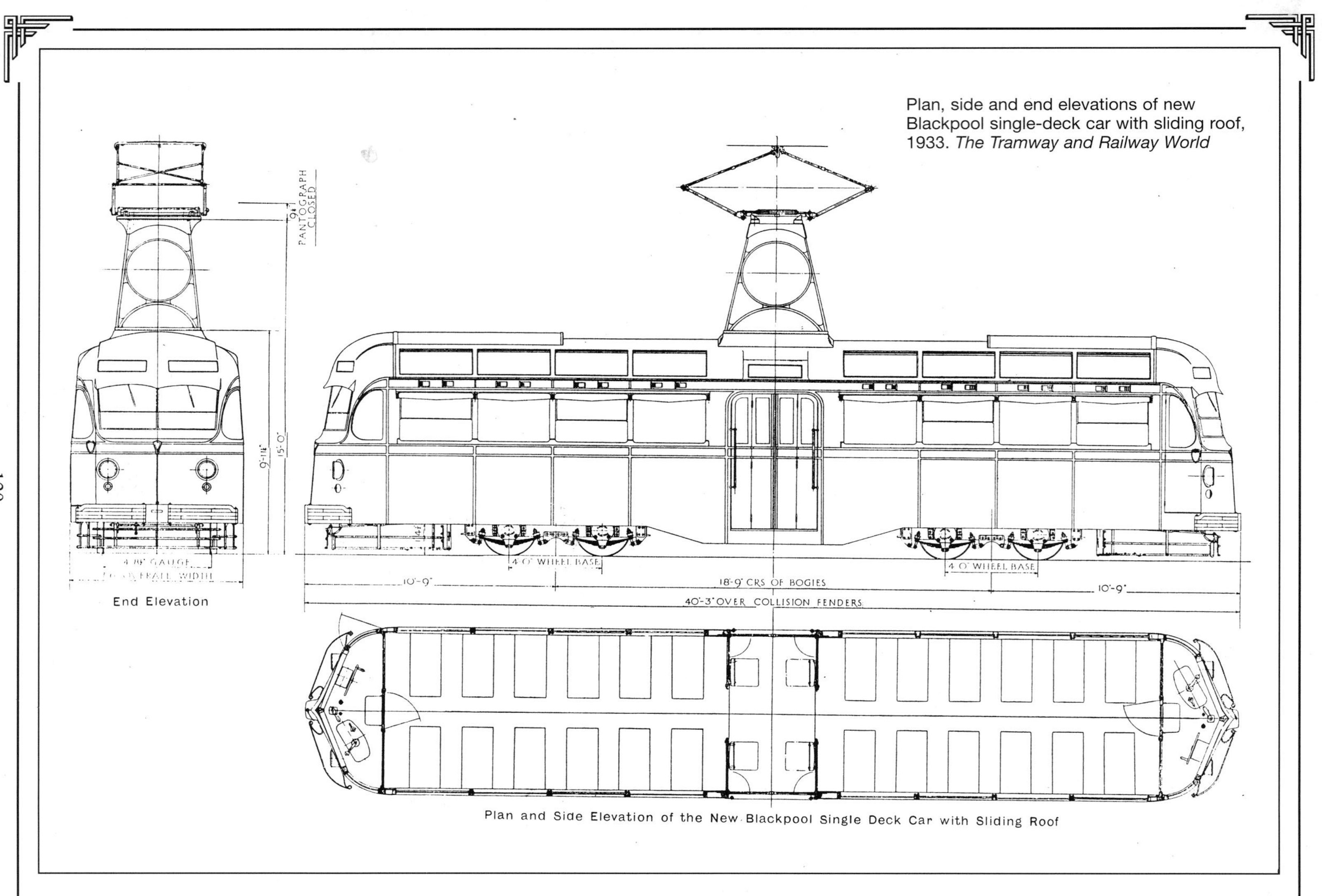

Plan, side and end elevations of new Blackpool single-deck car with sliding roof, 1933. *The Tramway and Railway World*

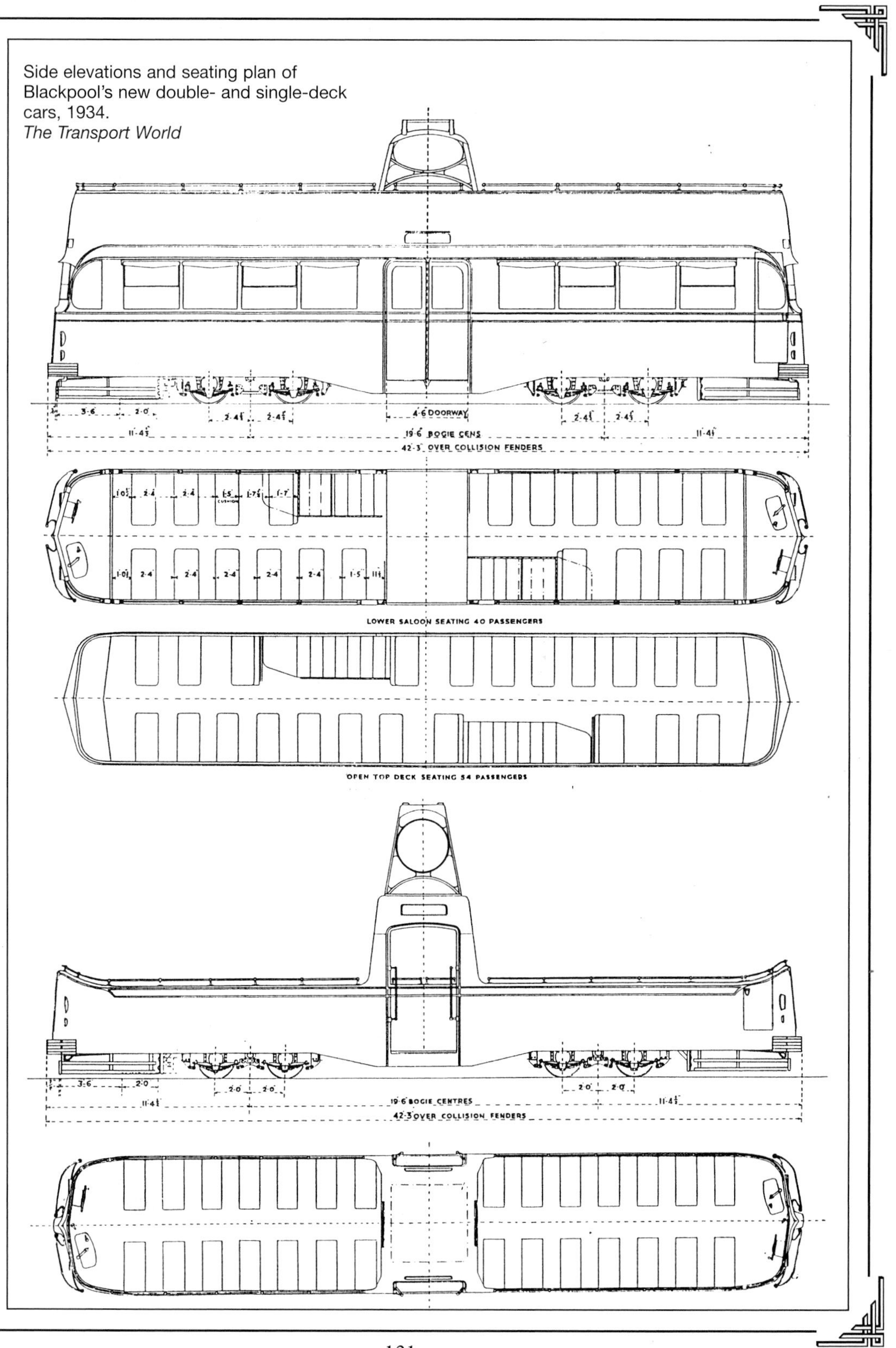

Side elevations and seating plan of Blackpool's new double- and single-deck cars, 1934. *The Transport World*

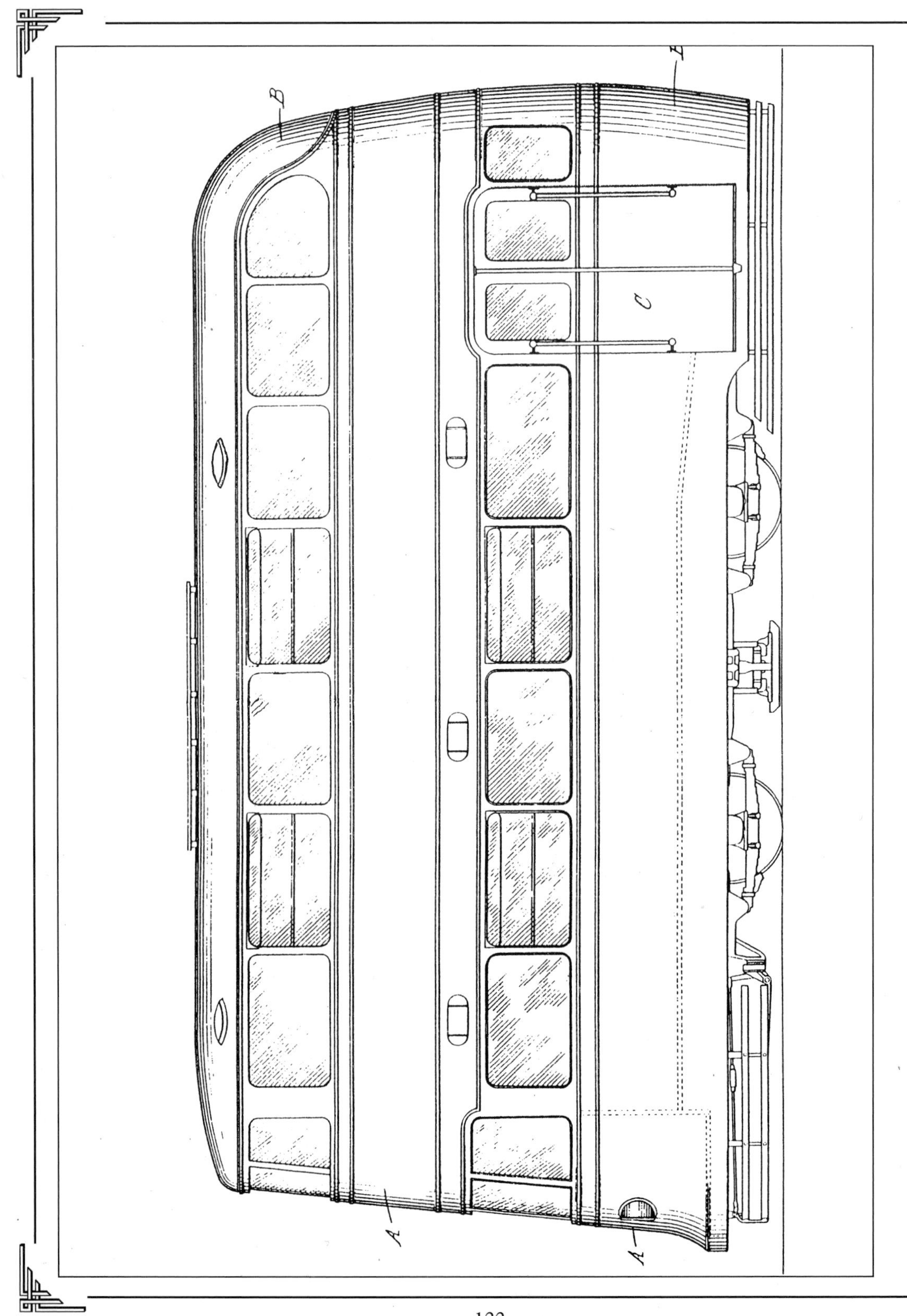
B
B
C
A
A

PATENT SPECIFICATION

422,091

Application Date: March 19, 1934. No. 8569/34.

Complete Specification Accepted: Jan. 4, 1935.

COMPLETE SPECIFICATION

Tramcar

We, THE ENGLISH ELECTRIC COMPANY LIMITED, a Company registered under British Law, of Queen's House, 28, Kingsway, London, W.C.2, and TOM PERCY SYKES, a British Subject, of 1, Eslaforde, Doncaster Road, Rotherham, Yorkshire, do hereby declare the nature of this invention and in what manner the same is to be performed, to be particularly described and ascertained in and by the following statement:—

The present invention lies in the novel shape imparted to a tramcar body whereby a striking appearance is given to a vehicle intended for uni-directional operation, by which latter expression is meant that the vehicle when in service for passenger carrying is driven only in one direction with respect to the vehicle, and it is not intended to exclude reversal for shunting and like purposes. Such a tramcar may have advantages in certain circumstances, such as for example on circular routes.

The invention lies in imparting to a longitudinally asymmetrical body a decided difference between the characteristic shapes of the ends. The body encloses the driver's compartment, that is to say, the walls of the upper and lower decks are substantially continuous around the front end and windows are employed making a substantially continuous exterior shape for the front, which is sloped upwardly and rearwardly as shown at A on the accompanying drawing, which represents in elevation a tramcar in accordance with the invention. The rear end is shaped as shown at B so as to present a convex outer surface enclosing the body, leaving no external passenger platform.

For a tramcar of this kind a single entrance and exit door will in general be found sufficient, situated on one side only and preferably towards the rear as shown at C.

Having now particularly described and ascertained the nature of our said invention, and in what manner the same is to be performed, we declare that what we claim is:—

1. A tramcar with a longitudinally saliently asymmetrical body enclosing the whole vehicle from end to end sloping upwardly and rearwardly at the front end and convex at the rear.

2. A tramcar as claimed in Claim 1 provided with a single entrance and exit on one side only situated towards the rear.

Dated this 6th day of March, 1934.

pp. The Applicants,
C. H. CLARKE,
Chartered Patent Agent,
107-110, Caxton House (East Block),
Westminster, London, S.W.1.

Leamington Spa: Printed for His Majesty's Stationery Office, by the Courier Press.—1935.

[*Price* 1/-]

Left and above: Drawing of No 422,091, including Patent specification.

Table 1

EE build list 1919. Orders passed to Preston by Electrical Traction Dept, Dick Kerr & Co Ltd, London

Order No	Date	Operator	Fleet Nos	Car Bodies	Top Covers Only
C1748	25.01.19	Morecambe Corp	14-5	2	
C10005	06.02.19	Southport Corp	29, 31, 33	3	
C10006	27.02.19	Nottingham Corp	?	12	
C10006	27.02.19	Nottingham Corp	?	-	2
C10011	01.03.19	Bradford Corp	233-58	26	
C10012	27.02.19	Huddersfield Corp	107-26	20	
C10013	06.03.19	Liverpool Corp	609-33	25	
C10015	10.03.19	Manchester Corp	798-835	38	
C10015	10.03.19	Manchester Corp	836-47	12	
C10016	06.03.19	Burton-upon-Trent Corp	21-4	4	
C10026	16.04.19	Doncaster Corp	38-47	10	
C10037	16.04.19	Nottingham Corp	156-80	25	
C10039	24.04.19	Lincoln Corp	9-11	3	
C10047	09.05.19	Yorkshire (West Riding)	various	8	
C10056	21.05.19	Wigan Corp	7-12	6	
C10065	29.05.19	Rotherham Corp	?	1	
C10065	29.05.19	Rotherham Corp	?	7	
C10065	29.05.19	Rotherham Corp	?	4	
C10073	26.05.19	TT&TC*	28-30	3	
C10073	16.10.19	TT&TC*	27	1	
C10115	05.06.19	Leicester Corp	167-78	12	
C10147	20.06.19	Southampton Corp	82-91	10	
C10162	24.06.19	Wolverhampton Corp	53-6	4	
C10162	24.06.19	Wolverhampton Corp	57-8	2	
C10196	03.11.19	South Shields Corp	41-5	5	
C10209	19.08.19	Oldham Corp	4-12, 14-6	12	
C10220	31.07.19	Dover Corp	25-7	3	
C10239	09.09.19	Stockport Corp	51-60	10	
C10268	26.08.19	Swindon Corp	13	1	
C10290	09.19	Sunderland Corp	72-7	6	
C10376	10.19	Bolton Corp	113-20	8	
C10410	06.10.19	Stockport Corp	61-5	5	
C10412	10.10.19	Portsmouth Corp	105-16	12	
C10483	21.11.19	Darwen Corp	20-2	3	
C10518	11.19	Ashton-under-Lyne Corp	27-38	12	
C10579	05.12.19	Rochdale Corp	70-9	10	
Column totals				**325**	**2**

*TT&TC — Tyneside Tramways & Tramroads Co

Table 2

EE build list 1920-2. Orders passed to Preston by English Electric Co Ltd, London

Order No	Date	Operator	Fleet Nos	Car Bodies	Top Covers Only
50099	20.04.20	Sunderland Corp	78-83	6	
50174	08.01.20	Bradford Corp	213-32	20	
50175	01.01.20	Manchester Corp	848-97	50	
50312	22.06.20	Colne Corp	2-3	2	
50408	18.02.20	Cheltenham & District Lt Rly Co	21-3	3	
50408	22.08.21	Leamington & Warwick	14	1	
50441	19.02.20	Nottingham Corp	?	15	
50582	27.04.20	Burnley Corp	68-72	5	
50661	08.03.20	Dumbarton	31-2	2	
51079	24.03.20	Llandudno & Colwyn Bay	19-22	4	
51322	30.03.20	St Helens Corp	18-21 (?)	-	4
51555	28.04.20	Llanelly & District	15-6	2	
52801	10.08.20	Wolverhampton Corp	59, 60-1	3	
52936	28.08.20	South Lancs Tramways Co	?	3	
52936	28.08.20	South Lancs Tramways Co	?	-	6
53320	11.10.20	South Lancs Tramways Co	?	-	4
53505	15.12.20	Northampton Corp	34-7	4	
54940	22.08.21	Dewsbury & Ossett	?	-	2
55359	19.01.22	Notts & Derby	1- 3	-	3
55453	09.03.22	Nottingham Corp	?	6	
55462	15.03.22	Morecambe Corp	13, 16	2	
Column totals				**128**	**19**

Right: The interior of the lower saloon on Aberdeen car No 141 was upholstered using a different pattern material from the one used in car No 139. The onset of World War 2 had not stopped these cars being finished to an extremely high standard. *EE*

Table 3

Build list. Orders dealt with by Tramways Section, Preston

Order No	Date	Operator	Fleet Nos	Car Bodies	Top Covers Only
5013	01.08.22	Liverpool Overhead Rly	?	-	1
5031	12.10.22	West Hartlepool Corp	8-9	2	
5056	11.01.23	Norwich Electric Tramways Co	7-8	2	
5071	12.03.23	Bolton Corp	121-30	10	
5077	24.04.23	Hull Corp	101	1	
5079	29.03.23	City of Carlisle ET Co Ltd	15	1	
5081	06.04.23	South Lancs Tramways Co	?	4	
5081	06.04.23	South Lancs Tramways Co	?	-	4
5088	30.05.23	Dearne District Light Railways	1-25	25	
5105	21.06.23	Nottingham Corp	?	10	
5106	28.07.23	Huddersfield Corp	127-36	10	
5114	15.08.23	Plymouth Corp	131-50	20	
5117	22.08.23	Lytham St Annes Borough	41-50	10	
5123	20.08.23	Salford Corp	151-60	-	10
5128	11.01.24	Oldham Corp	17-20, 22, 24	6	
5158	14.01.24	SSCP*	56-61	6	
5160	18.01.24	Edinburgh Corp	312-31	20	
5170	20.02.24	Norwich Electric Tramways Co	43-5, 47	4	
5177	05.03.24	South Lancs Tramways Co	?	3	
5177	05.03.24	South Lancs Tramways Co	?	-	4
5196	26.05.24	Bolton Corp	?	-	4
5200	03.06.24	Dearne District Light Railways	26-30	5	
5203	26.08.24	Rochdale Corp	80-5	6	
5211	12.07.24	Nottingham Corp	?	12	
5222	16.09.24	SSCP*	18-23	-	6
5223	16.09.24	York Corp	37	1	
5230	26.09.24	Norwich Electric Tramways Co	4, 23, 33, 38-9, 41	6	
5233	29.10.24	SSCP*	24-5, 37-9	-	5
5245	17.03.25	West Ham Corp Tramways	119-24	6	
5259	04.03.25	Manchester Corp	934-93	60	
5263	03.03.25	Dewsbury & Ossett	?	-	6
5270	21.04.25	City of Carlisle ET Co Ltd	14	1	
5275	25.05.25	Bury Corp	55-60	6	
5275	25.05.25	Bury Corp	1-6 (?)	-	6
5283	23.06.25	Mansfield & District Light Rly Co	27-8	2	
5302-1	27.10.25	Rochdale Corp	86-9	4	
5302-2	27.10.25	Rochdale Corp	90-2	3	
5303	03.11.25	Norwich Electric Tramways Co	1-3, 8, 13, 24	6	
5305	28.10.25	Bolton Corp	8-10	3	
5309	02.11.25	Oldham Corp	121-32	12	
5313	24.11.25	Leeds City Tramways	76-150	75	
5326	02.03.26	Bury Corp	7-14 (?)	-	8
5337	12.04.26	Nottingham Corp	181-200	20	

*SSCP — Southend-on-Sea Corp

Right: Aberdeen had to wait until 1946 before it could place its order for a further 20 bogie cars. This time, the bodies were built by a subcontractor, R. Y. Pickering & Co at Wishaw. No 20, one of the cars built by them, is seen at Bridge of Don on 3 March 1951. *M. H. Waller, courtesy A. W. Brotchie*

Order No	Date	Operator	Fleet Nos	Car Bodies	Top Covers Only
5343	16.08.26	Manchester Corp	1004-53	50	
5350	13.07.26	Rochdale Corp	93	-	1
5352	13.08.26	Bolton Corp	139-50	12	
5369	02.11.26	Norwich Electric Tramways Co	6, 17-8, 29	4	
5377	17.01.27	South Lancs Tramways	44-5	2	
5414	21.10.27	Norwich Electric Tramways Co	15, 25, 40, 42	4	
5426	17.02.28	Blackpool Corp	167-76	10	
5457	24.07.28	Rochdale Corp	94	-	1
5458	07.28	Liverpool Corp	757	1	
5459	07.28	Coventry Corp	64-8	5	
5463	05.08.28	Bolton Corp	104-6	3	
5468	24.10.28	London County Council	552-601	50	
5478	07.01.29	Halifax Corp	114-20	7	
5485	18.01.29	Norwich Electric Tramways Co	10-1, 14, 33	4	
5513	04.10.29	London County Council	1854-903	50	
5526	22.11.29	Halifax Corp	121-3	3	
5531	08.11.29	Norwich Electric Tramways Co	20, 26	2	
5543	26.02.30	Rochdale Corp	3, 10-1, 29-30	-	5
5543	26.02.30	Rochdale Corp	44-9	-	6
5568	27.05.30	Manx Electric Railway	40-1, 44	3	
5575	04.08.30	Norwich Electric Tramways Co	22, 34	2	
5591	24.10.30	Liverpool Corp	758-69	*	
5600	27.11.30	London County Council	161-210	50	
5609	20.05.31	Huddersfield Corp	137-42	6	
5676	01.06.32	Huddersfield Corp	143-4	2	
57xx	11.32	Sunderland Corp	87-95	9	
5730	20.03.33	Blackpool Corp	200	1	
57xx	07.33	Edinburgh Corp	262-3, 267	3	
5752	15.08.33	Blackpool Corp	201-24	24	
5758	02.11.33	Blackpool Corp	226	1	
5762	15.11.33	Blackpool Corp	225	1	
Column totals				**671**	**63**

* Motor equipments and bogies only

Table 3

EE build list 1934-46. Orders dealt with by Tramways Section, Bradford

Order No	Date	Operator	Fleet Nos	Car Bodies	Top Covers Only
4D 0012	01.34	Blackpool Corp	226-36	11	
6D 0014	19.02.34	Blackpool Corp	250-63	14	
6D 0015	19.02.34	Blackpool Corp	238-49	12	
6D 0018	24.02.34	Sunderland Corp	99	1	
?	02.34	Rotherham Corp	1-6	6	
?	02.34	Leeds City Tramways	264-71	8	
?	06.34	Belfast Corp	392, 423-41	20	
?	12.34	Edinburgh Corp	19-24	6	
6E 0086	12.03.35	Blackpool Corp	264-83	20	
?	03.35	Rotherham Corp	7-11	5	
6E 0158	18.11.35	Darwen Corp	23-4	2	
6F 0169	01.36	Sunderland Corp	53	1	
?	02.37	Glasgow Corp	1143-242	*	
6G 0289	07.06.37	Sunderland Corp	49-51	3†	
?	12.38	Glasgow Corp	1243-92	*	
6K 0382	02.39	Blackpool Corp	10-21	12	
6K 0384	11.04.39	Sunderland Corp	52	1†	
4K 0167	06.39	Aberdeen Corp	138-9	2	
4K 0167	06.39	Aberdeen Corp	140-1	2	
?	02.09.46	Aberdeen Corp	19-38	20	
Column total				**146**	

*Underframes and lower saloon frames only

†Supplied as kits of parts

Total of all tables			**1,270**	**84**
	Plus	30 Belfast to EEC drgs by Service Motor Works		
		150 Glasgow underframes and lower saloon frames		
		12 Liverpool built to EEC drgs (?) by Liverpool		
		12 Wigan built to EEC drgs by Massey